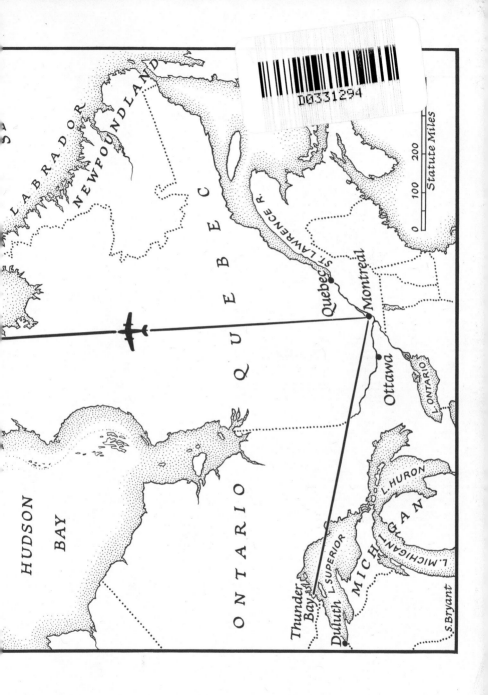

Books by Sheila Burnford

THE INCREDIBLE JOURNEY
THE FIELDS OF NOON
WITHOUT RESERVE
ONE WOMAN'S ARCTIC

ONE
WOMAN'S
ARCTIC

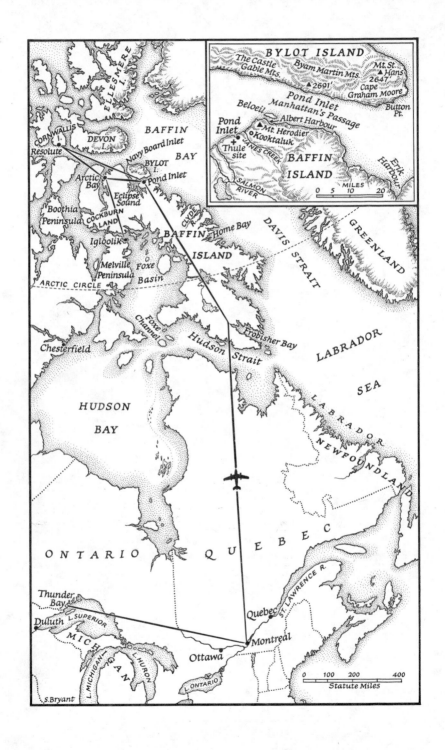

ONE
WOMAN'S
ARCTIC

by Sheila Burnford

AN ATLANTIC MONTHLY PRESS BOOK

Little, Brown and Company · Boston · Toronto

FIRST AMERICAN EDITION

T07/73

Library of Congress Cataloging in Publication Data

Burnford, Sheila (Every)
On woman's Arctic.

"An Atlantic Monthly Press book."
Includes bibliographical references.
1. Eskimos--Baffin Island.   I. Title.
E99.E7B92 1973   970.4'12'9   73-3417
ISBN 0-316-11716-1

ATLANTIC—LITTLE, BROWN BOOKS
ARE PUBLISHED BY
LITTLE, BROWN AND COMPANY
IN ASSOCIATION WITH
THE ATLANTIC MONTHLY PRESS

PRINTED IN THE UNITED STATES OF AMERICA

FOR J. D. L.

I will walk with leg muscles
which are strong
as the sinews of the little caribou calf.
I will walk with leg muscles
which are strong
as the sinews of the little hare.
   I will take care not to go towards the dark
   I will go towards the day.

Eskimo poem
translated by Knud Rasmussen

Acknowledgments

The author makes grateful acknowledgment to the following:

The Canada Council of Arts.
John and Colly Scullion, Heidi and Rick Hamburg, Jan Swietlik, Father Guy Mary-Rousselière, and all those other helpful and hospitable people, both Inuit and Kabloonah, of Pond Inlet.
Douglas Heyland, who made the greater snowgeese not only possible but comprehensible.
Willard Trask, who hacked his way so nobly through an ill-spelled, illegible, and comma-less jungle of manuscript.
Jean Briggs, for permission to quote from her thesis, "Utkuhiksalingmiut: Eskimo Emotional Expressions, the Patterning of Affection and Hostility," Harvard University, 1967.

ONE
WOMAN'S
ARCTIC

☙ *Chapter 1* ☙

"The pilot, who was an Eskimo," I wrote in a journal that June evening,

flew low over open water at one point, on a level with a rounded bastion of striated cliffs, and there below us, like white submarines cruising along, was a pod of beluga whales. Later we came down even lower; he pointed down, and I could make out quite clearly huge tracks leading back from the floe edge, and following them back and back, they suddenly resolved into a defined form, and there was one brief unforgettable glimpse of a polar bear.

We must have been passing over Lancaster Sound then, en route from Resolute Bay, close to the north magnetic pole, to Pond Inlet, an Eskimo settlement on northeast Baffin. It was like nothing I had ever imagined the high Arctic to be, not a flat white endless expanse, but an incredible grandeur of mountains and ice-locked fjords, and frozen, patterned seas — and color:

Sometimes there were long black openings in the ice, sometimes by the shoreline glass green circles of water on the ice, brilliant blues and aquas in icebergs; great glaciers like white highways, terminating in wild upheavals of glacial moraine on the shoreline.

The aircraft was a twin-engined Otter, with canvas folding seats, wreaths of tobacco smoke drifting out of the cockpit, a pile of freight and baggage in the rear, and six other passengers: a young Eskimo woman, with a baby asleep in the hood of her white duck amouti; a small dark man; and four French Canadians, members of a construction crew, three of them still sleeping off the monumental hangovers with which they had embarked at Montreal two days before. Then they were all strangers — Markoosie, the pilot; Elizee, with whom we would go narwhal hunting; Dorcasee, whose portrait with her new baby would adorn the kindergarten walls; or Louis Domina, the cook, who was to slip us onions and freshly baked bread; or Gilles; or . . . But they were as yet unnamed faces in the colorful group standing around when the Otter came down on the airstrip cut out of the flat hill behind Pond — smiling, animated faces, a warm reddy brown in the mellow sunlight of nearly midnight, the Inuit, the "people."

And we were then strangers to them, not just as people but as to purpose, for most people who come to Pond come on some specialized Arctic reason. Furthermore, they are usually of a younger generation. We were two Kabloonahs, white women *d'un certain âge*, as the French so happily put it, with grownup families. Susan's purpose was immediately obvious, as they unloaded all the paraphernalia of a painter — she was there to work for a forthcoming exhibition of Indian and Eskimo paintings at the Royal Ontario Museum. I was there just "to be there," as I had vaguely put it when giving reasons why I should apply for a grant toward expenses from the Canada Council. We had combined our interests in this kind of expedition many times before in some of the most northerly Indian reserves in Ontario, and had found that it worked out very well, both going our own ways, yet each finding our eyes and ears complemented by the impressions of those of the other. Now, after many years of making friends and being accepted among the Ojibwa and Crees, we hoped to spend the spring and summer along the same lines in an Eskimo settlement. As I had written once in a book describing those Indian experiences, we came "neither to exhort or teach, heal, snoop, pay or persuade, but in peace alone, in friendly interest, to learn something of their language and life." And where compatible — I might have added, if pressed to elaborate on just "being there" — to further my own mild amateur interests in birds and wild flowers, animals and artifacts.

Through the years of going north we had learned to settle for anything in the way of accommodation — fur shack, nursing station, a tent if need be — and had had no idea what Pond would be able to produce; somewhere large enough, we hoped, to hold Susan's prospective models at the same time as us and our sleeping bags. A mattress for the latter would be a nice refinement, and a stove of some kind, with a pot or pan or two perhaps, possibly even the loan of a table. But other than that our sights were not aimed any higher.

We are in Paradise [I wrote that night] and think every now and then of various friends and relations who imagine us eating blubber in an igloo and suffering untold privations of cold and rugged living.

Paradise was the kindergarten, a most spacious building of the government hostel type, on the height at the far end of the village. Because of the permafrost, its foundations were raised high above the ground, with entrances on either side up a flight of stairs. The one village road passed the windows at the back, and below the front windows the hill sloped down to the frozen strait between Baffin and the spectacular Castle Gable range of Bylot Island. Not only were there two bathrooms, but there was a well-equipped kitchen with an oil stove, and two cots with comfortable mattresses had been put in a front room. As for the hoped-for loan of a table — there were tables everywhere, gnome-sized, admittedly, with gnome-sized chairs to match, but sensibly shaped to be pushed together to form one enormous whole, or two large rounds, so that we could each lay claim to surface space. Everything was wonderfully light, with the reflection from the ice and the clean, yellow color inside, and was to remain flooded in sunlight twenty-four hours a day.

At the moment there was still a week of school to go, when the children would be coming in the mornings, but after that we would have the entire run of the place, complete with toys, Plasticine, chalks, a miniature kitchen, and neatly printed cards all round telling us that this was a DOOR, this a WINDOW, here was the place to take off our BOOTS, with a picture showing us how to do this. Soon our own language attempts were to join these cards; usefully social phrases written large in red crayon, so that we could practice them in our goings-out and comings-in: INGE-LUKTIT — please sit down. KINAUOOVIT? — what is your name? AMAH-LOO PULONYIA LOWIT — please come again, all transcribed in our own phonetic version of the language. One phrase we were to find useless — "Come in" — for no one ever knocked at a door; they just opened it and came in. As they are a quiet people to start with, and usually wore soft, silent kamiks, the sealskin boots, it took a little while to get used to waking up to find a smiling face peering round the bedroom or bathroom door, or suddenly materializing at one's elbow at almost any time of day or night.

It took a little while as well to get used to the timelessness of the twenty-four-hour days of high summer, with the sun circling the sky with equal brilliance at midday or midnight, although at first there was a clear distinction when the sleepy little four- or five-year-olds arrived at 9 A.M. for school — sleepy because most of them had probably been up until the early hours. Now there was a curfew to ensure some rest for schoolchildren; later on they would be playing out on the ice on the slopes below my window at any time: five o'clock at night or five o'clock in the morning, there was always someone about.

We owed Paradise to the thoughtfulness of the Area Administration, to John Scullion, who was the Administrator, and Rick Hamburg, his assistant. There was only one official place for nonresidents in Pond, and that was the Transient Center next door, four-bunks-to-a-room type of accommodation, for the construction crews or weatherbound geologists and other Arctic wayfarers; so someone had come up with the inspired idea of renting the kindergarten under the auspices of the Toonoonik Sahoonin Council, the Eskimo Cooperative. Bernadette, the attractive Eskimo wife of Leigh Brintnell, the school principal, was to run the scheme. She even managed to produce a nice little girl called Lily, who wandered in from time to time to clean the place. Lily in turn produced her grandmother, who made wonderful stone dolls, and her grandmother produced a relative, Kuminahpik, who made the best ooloos — the women's curved knives. And so it went on indefinitely; everyone in Pond, it seemed, was related in one way or another.

My bed was directly under the window, looking across to the mountains and glaciers of Bylot Island, some twenty miles away, and if ever I come back to haunt some place it will be that window, for I never tired of looking out of it. The world out there changed from minute to minute, color, light and sound. Now the strait was ice-locked to silence and there were no birds; soon there would be the sound of open water and shifting, groaning, creaking ice floes, the air filled with the music of dozens of different gulls and waterfowl. Now the rocky hillside was covered in snow; in a few days it would spring into brilliant life, carpeted with myriad wild flowers. One moment the glaciers opposite would seem remote as another continent; next time I looked it would seem that I only had to walk a mile or so

across the ice to be at the end of their thousands-of-years-old
road. Or the mountains would be cloud-wreathed, the sun striking in silver shafts across the ice below; then a pure white peak
from the ice cap would rear through the clouds, catch the sun,
and so change light and color again.

Every year, at the end of the brief Arctic summer, the giant
icebergs that had calved in Milne Inlet came sailing past the
settlement, one after another, in every imaginable shape and
form, from turreted castles and pyramids to skyscrapers and
battleships. As the procession sailed back and forth, in a tantalizing display driven by wind and tide, the excitement mounted
among those who had a favorite, for always one berg was held
captive for the year on a reef immediately opposite the village.
This year's was a splendid affair, guaranteed to please everyone,
as not only was it spectacularly towering, but it had all kinds of
intricate ice sculpture and differing levels as well, so that the
sun striking the varying angles and prisms of ice changed its
shape and color all the time.

The ice before the settlement's shoreline was never empty of
interest or excitement either: now it would be a dog team coming in, or a skidoo — a mechanized toboggan — going out, the
long sleds (which we soon learned to call komatiks) piled high
with all the equipment of the hunters. There were six or seven
dog teams staked out there when we first arrived, and several
more around the point, and at all times of the day or night they
would lift their voices to provide the background music of Pond
— the most dramatic and nostalgic sound to me in the world,
the great swelling chorus of huskies singing, voice after voice
taking up the song, until the last diminuendos, usually ending
with a tremulous solo. After a while I was able to recognize
different songs — the excitement of greeting a returning team,
or of an approaching owner, the first cut of a knife into their
seal dinner, mild boredom, or just time for a sing over nothing

in particular. They howled sitting or standing, and if standing, with tails raised high. Soon it was possible to isolate individual voices. Almost from the first night by that magical window I started taping a Husky Opera with a small recorder I had rolled up in my sleeping bag at the very last moment, hanging the microphone outside the open window, the recorder by the pillow. Thus, if a particularly stirring operatic moment was reached in the middle of the night, or if the soprano I had earmarked for the lead role was in good voice, all I had to do was switch on. It became an even more absorbing pastime when the ice started to break up, and broken-off floes with an entire dog team still staked out would sail off down the strait to the west, returning hours later when the pack ice was reformed by currents and tide. Then there could be some wonderful Pinkerton-Butterfly effects, if my soprano happened to be aboard a departing ice floe, and Pinkerton was still stationary, or staked out on the hillside. Then, of course, if I could tape some of the libretto against a simultaneous chorus of old squaw ducks — who really deserved an opera to themselves — or red-throated divers, it was a real triumph.

There was only one road in Pond; sandy and deeply rutted in places, it followed the shoreline for about three quarters of a mile from the Anglican mission at one end of the village, across a river, to climb uphill to the headland just beyond the kindergarten. Halfway, like the stem of an inverted T, it climbed steeply to the airstrip on a plateau between the rising hills. Traffic at its never-yet-achieved peak, in total Pond Inlet strength, could consist of the Bombardier (a kind of workhorse minibus on tractor treads), the water tractor, the garbage tractor and one other — and Bernadette in her Volkswagen, the first and only car to be seen in northern Baffin. It had been brought in by the annual sealift the year before, and had done quite a bit of mileage on the ice during the winter. It was on this busy thoroughfare that Bernadette had taken her driving license test, and got it at one go (despite the hazard of the water truck making its morning rounds), through a community effort of Pat King, the Mountie, conducting the test, and John Scullion, in his dual capacity of Area Administrator and Justice of the Peace, issuing the license.

Sooner or later during the day, up and down this road, passed the entire community, conveniently close to the back windows of the kindergarten. It was a most colorful community, for one of the pleasantest surprises was the manner in which it still dressed. Up until now, when I had seen photographs of Eskimos in furs or sealskin or in amoutis with babies peeping over their shoulders, I had thought it was probably a gimmick for the photographer — like Indians getting themselves up in feathers and buckskin for the tourists. Almost everyone wore what I used to think of as being mukluks, but which were called kamiks here: three-quarter-length boots made either entirely of sealskin, or, and more commonly at this time of year, white duck and sealskin, the tassels of brightly colored drawstrings at the back. These were drawn over long, thick, white duffle or blanket cloth underkamiks, the turned-down tops embroidered all round, mostly with flowers. Almost all the women, and very often little girls as well, wore the white amoutis, the loose, knee-length overgarment with the ingeniously designed deep pouch hood. Usually they were made from closely woven, windproof white duck, although occasionally it would be duffle. The individual variation in these was achieved in the wide braids that crossed over the chest, some of them being exquisitely embroidered, and in the colors of the wool tassels of the long girdle. Knee length, with an even hem, seemed to be traditional in Pond, but there were a few women coming from other parts who wore the swallow-tailed amouti, the scoop of the "tail" coming almost to the ankles. Below the amoutis individual tastes ranged wildly — from the swinging, bell-bottom trousers of the young women to the thick woolen stockings and cotton dresses of their mothers.

The men were more conservative, with store-bought trousers tucked into their kamiks (although a few older men wore white duffle trousers on Sundays), and Grenfell cloth parkas over duffle-lined jackets — the material being bought at the Hudson Bay store, then made to most careful measurements where the hood joined the shoulders, and finally embroidered around the hem and sleeves, again either in flowers or with strips of colored braid. Dog fur rimmed the hoods, ranging from white to black to ginger.

The destination of the passersby, if they were not just out visiting, was the Hudson Bay store. The store and the Royal Canadian Mounted Police post had been built alongside one another about fifty years ago, only a few yards separating them from the beach. Both were gleaming white, with Maple Leaves fluttering from the flagposts, the paths marked by whitewashed boulders (the latter one of the hard labor tasks in the unlikely event of anyone serving time at Pond). The Mounties had little to do locally (the only crime that happened while I was there was someone "borrowing" the administrative skidoo and taking it off on a joy ride), and were often to be seen whitewashing their own particular section of boulders. During my first year they were still running the post office, and I used to go there just for the joy and wonderment of getting my banal stamps from someone who looked like all the *Boys Own Paper* models of jutting-jawed, crew-cut, piercingly blue-eyed Mounties rolled into one. Occasionally they took off in an RCMP aircraft, if not to get their man, at least to see that peace was reigning in their farther-flung territories, and the game laws being observed. The year before, the last RCMP dog team had been disbanded, and some of the beautiful, pure strain huskies were to be seen around in the village. A gleaming skidoo, with a komatik painted in RCMP blue, was now staked outside instead. The mail was supposed to come once a week on the regular "sked" flight from Resolute, but its arrival was as uncertain as the weather conditions. Otherwise, communication with the outside world was by radiotelephone. A large proportion of houses had telephones hooked up on the village's own system.

The store was run by Alec, traditionally Scottish, and married to a local Eskimo woman. He had a young white assistant, and either Merkasiak or his daughter Tabitha were behind the counter to tot up purchases, which could range from rifles and ammunition, furs and stoves to patent medicines, framed pictures (frightful Highland cattle or Indian-maid-in-canoe), toys, and clothes, besides the usual tinned and packaged food. By June the shelves were very bare, for the year's supply was coming to its end before the August sealift, when the supply boat and oil tanker were able to anchor in the opened water offshore. As with the handful of white residents in Pond, who had to make out their shopping lists a year ahead, some careful commissioning was required, as supplies that had run out or been forgotten had to be freighted in by air at a dollar a pound. The Eskimo people of Pond had a community deepfreeze hut for fish, seal, caribou, etc. — making somewhat of a nonsense of the old joke about selling refrigerators to Eskimos.

Used to the ramshackle houses of the northern Indians, dotted about at random around a settlement, I found the tidy layout of the houses here a revelation. They were mostly of the standard prefabricated government type, the "crackerbox" one room, and its larger cousins with two or three bedrooms. They had large windows and slightly sloping roofs, usually festooned with caribou antlers, sealskin frames or furs. All were oil-heated; water came from big, plastic tanks filled from the water tank; and sanitation was the standard model for a land where no subsoil

drainage is possible — an oversize green garbage bag lining a
pail and crowned with a plastic seat. The white people, the
Kabloonahs, had a somewhat more elaborate version, plus a
bathroom, the exception being the nursing station, which con-
sisted of two trailers. Colors of houses varied according to individual whim.

Mainly that first week — and, indeed, almost all of the weeks
that were to follow, that first year — was one of impressions:
like a piece of blotting paper I simply absorbed whatever came
my way, content to be given bits of information, not to question
or inquire, more interested in the land, and in the people as villagers and friendly faces, than in their relationships, or in the
workings and economy of the settlement.

Smells — how could I have left them out of the list of important first impressions, for they are the most evocative of all,
their initial impact never again so strong. Pond for me is forever
associated with the slightly sickly sweet, but not altogether
unpleasant, smell of blubber, particularly when it was emerging
from the snow to the warmth of the sun along the shore and on
the rocks. Everywhere that dogs had been staked out, the left-
over blubber from many seal carcasses glued to unwary boots.
And everywhere there was blubber, there was other thawing
evidence of the dogs — only to rank in first impression importance, thereafter to be accepted and forgotten, except in re-
reading this very early entry in my journal:

"One could write a fascinating thesis on dog turds alone here:
they abound everywhere, and are at first the thing one is most
conscious of on the landscape. On the ice particularly, for every
small, deep, round pool of water has been formed around one,
and they are magnified by the water. The contents aren't a bit
unpleasant, but fascinating: caribou hairs predominate, scraps
of leather or canvas harness, red duffle, sealskin, and one stun-

ningly exotic offering that looked like a strip of nylon lace."
But at least they were confined to the ice and shoreline and
adjacent hillside, as Kyak, the special constable, had the authority to round up any loose offenders in the village itself, and if
necessary, shoot them if they were not claimed. Their carcasses
were quite a feature of the landscape too.

Cats were not in evidence that first year. There had been one,
brought in by one of the teachers. Then someone had recently
thought it must be a very lonely life for her, and brought in
from Arctice Bay, several hundred miles away, by Bombardier, a
ginger tom. He now lived at one end of the village, she at the
other, and they had not yet met, but hopes were high that this
would be the foundation of a great Arctic cat dynasty.

Each day as I wandered along the village street, barred from
further exploring by the snow on the hills and shores, faces
resolved into personalities, some clearer than others, but all so
friendly and welcoming that it was impossible to feel shy or a
stranger for long. Already many of them had been in and out of
the kindergarten, to sit for portraits, or just to visit. Many of
them we came to know through the kindergarten children, for
by now all the names laboriously printed on the works of art
adorning the walls had become live: Ahseetah, Koonah, Joeli,
Simonee, Oorootah, Malachai were some of them; quiet, round-
eyed, little people, with pinky-brown, glowing cheeks, who
barely spoke above a whisper, but who could giggle enchant-
ingly when they played a game like the Hunter and the Five
Foxes, where the "foxes" ended up by being shot and then
skinned (i.e., tickled). Jan Swietlik, their teacher, said that the
attention span of these children was far longer than that of any
white child she had taught: they were capable at five years old
of sitting quite still and concentrating for at least three quarters
of an hour, and were really unhappy if school ended to interrupt
a project — such as a painting unfinished — and would even

sneak back in and finish it if possible. It was their incredible accuracy and coordination that fascinated me; anything delicate or complex could be left out without any fears of breakage: they might pick it up, examine it minutely, then replace it exactly with their small deft hands. Little boys outside, not more than three or four, would play for hours with a miniature dog whip, the lash nevertheless being about fifteen feet, curling it back then flicking the target of a stone or a stick.

I watched a three-year-old at the bay one day. His father had just bought him a double-barreled pop-gun. The child unwrapped it there and then from its plastic cover — no hurried tearing apart to get at it — then fitted the corks into the barrels, very carefully and accurately, tamping them in with tiny competent fingers; and when one seemed a bit tight, he licked it carefully before pushing it in with a screwing movement. His father had to "break" the gun for him to set the spring, as it was too stiff, then he went outside and stood on the steps, sighted carefully, and pulled the trigger, a perfect miniature hunter in his kamiks and parka. The smallest child in Pond would wield a knife, whether scimitar or pocket-sized, without any adult being alarmed.

Bringing their smaller brothers and sisters — even a baby in a little girl's amouti — they often came back to the kindergarten after school, hoping to be drawn by Susan, always extremely polite and well behaved, carefully removing their boots under the BOOTS sign before coming in. The doors were never locked, and we never thought of putting anything away, for they would never have thought of taking anything.

The kindergarten was one of the most imaginative and well equipped that I have ever been in. Equally, the school proper next door lacked no facility. The spaciousness and light were a revelation, including an assembly hall large enough for the full wide-screen showing there of the weekly films for the community. Obviously a great deal of money and thought had been expended on the education of Eskimo children. It was difficult not to contrast what I found here with a school in an equally isolated Indian settlement in northern Ontario. Even the primary readers showed some thought; instead of the trite irrelevancies of a Dick and Jane and dog Rover in some white suburbia, the pictures here all had to do with something familiar to an Eskimo child: mother — anana, father — atata, seal — natsimut, kukijuk — gun; thus atata kukereartuk natsimut — father shoots seal — with a nice clear picture of father doing just that.

Next year, apparently, the Northwest Territories Schools Board hoped to introduce more and more schoolbooks written and illustrated by the Eskimos themselves, all part of a new curriculum more heavily weighted to a policy of retaining the Eskimo culture and language. To this end Soolah, one of the most interesting women in the village, had already been enlisted as a kindergarten assistant, to tell the traditional stories of her people and teach their games. The Schools Board had suddenly awakened to the fact that, with compulsory education, a culture was vanishing, the time and opportunity for stories and games within the home itself being no longer there. Nor, soon, will there be the skills, for a son no longer has the free time to accompany his father out hunting, nor a daughter the time to assist her mother in the preparation of sealskin and caribou for clothes and kamiks.

Soolah was Bernadette's mother, and if ever there is a demand for a native Canadian female Prime Minister, she will be my candidate. In fact, she was not unlike a small Mrs. Golda Meir in appearance:

In the afternoon I went to Soolah's house (immaculate, and the usual Sony tape recorder and powerful radio); she small and gap-toothed, with steel-rimmed glasses and a wonderful smile, and very patient with my pronunciation when she was teaching me to count. She was sewing intricate appliqués in sealskin with caribou sinew, and is going to make me short sealskin kamiks. She is quite a formidable figure on the council, I gather. Extremely intelligent, unusually direct, and is a lot in demand by Kabloonahs wishing to learn the language, or anthropologists tracking down folklore. Felt rather in awe of her — a few more like her around, with their feet on firm ground between the cultures, and the Eskimos are assured of their place in the modern world.

That was a first impression. It remained constant, if anything enhanced by further acquaintance.

Then there was Koonah, of the same matriarchal stuff, but a generation further back, child, mother and grandmother in nomadic days, yet seemingly perfectly adjusted now to a life within four centrally heated walls:

Met Koonah today, who is reputed to be the oldest woman on Baffin — probably about seventy-six. A sweet old girl, about four feet six inches, with doll-sized hands and feet. Sitting like a little girl on her bed, with her feet dangling, perfect sight, and very limber. Everything stowed away tidily in boxes under her bed, and on a shelf above it, along with a signed photograph "To Koonah" from the Governor General. Her one room crackerbox, shining clean and tidy, and she spitting tidily into an empty Klim tin. Strange that in that house there was no sign whatsoever of her own heritage, the only decoration on the wall a fan of flattened cigarette packets, yet in white houses here everyone has more than their quota of stone carvings, artifacts of every description, sealskin rugs, Eskimo prints etc. The Inuit prefer nice shiny linoleum, plastic flowers and Hudson Bay knives.

I learned that Koonah paid the government $6 a month, the minimum, rent for her house, which included the heating fuel and the complete standard furnishings and equipment of all Pond houses — beds, bunks, tables, chairs, sets of cutlery, plastic dinnerware and all kitchen utensils, down to the last eggbeater. The houses were light and comfortable and warm, but once or twice I heard the women say that it would have been better if they had had a say in the design: they didn't like all the compartmentalization into little bedroom-boxes, for they had been used to the family being all together in one tent, or igloo or sodhouse. The rents varied according to the resident's means and the number of bedrooms, the maximum being $67 per month (three bedrooms) from someone in the best paid employment.

Inoogah was the same age, and this was the first year that he had lived permanently in a settlement, coming in from his camp at Ickpeagyuk, many miles down the Baffin coast, because he said he felt he "was no longer strong enough to lift oil barrels by himself." Yet at seventy-six, he had bulging biceps like a man in his prime:

He is deeply religious, and told me he has read the Bible every day of his life since he was a boy, and has been through it many times now. When I came past, he and Martha, his wife, were sitting side by side on the steps of their house, both sawing and banging at chunks of soapstone. They are the only couple one sees continuously together. She gives a curiously avant-garde impression, from her unusually narrow head angled forward on a long neck, to her thin, amazingly supple legs, which are usually tucked under her as she perches on the table or chair — she would not look out of place in a Chelsea basement — and the Oriental planes of her sallow face. She is half the age of Inoogah, with a lively eye; perhaps that is why he looks a little haggard and harassed sometimes.

Most men had a biblical name, Levi, Joshua, Timothy, Samuel; very often "ee" or "usee" was added, thus: Markusee, Paulusee, Jobee. Sometimes the choice was a little unnerving — "That's Lazarus on the phone," said Colly Scullion to John one evening. "He wants to speak to you." ("And how is he feeling now?" one wanted to say.) Or Elijah — he was leaving about five o'clock,

I heard someone say the first time I heard his name; but by skidoo, to go hunting, it turned out — not running to catch the five o'clock Chariot of Fire. Many of the women, too, had biblical names, but there were Annies and Lilys and Lenas as well. But apart from the names, there has been very little infiltration of English words, or corruptions of them, into the Eskimo language. Usually it is a literal translation of meaning: a telephone, for example, is translated into "the instrument for speaking," a radio becomes "the instrument from which voices and music are heard." Skidoo was the nearest corruption I heard, becoming "Sic-a-doo."

This, then, was the village of Pond (population four hundred Inuit, about fifteen Kabloonahs), as much as I knew of it in the first week or so: only a few hundred miles from the North Pole, yet a complete, self-contained little cluster of buildings, with electric light, central heating, running water and even its own telephone system, set in some of the most magnificent scenery of the high Arctic — or the world, for that matter. Its people were self-sufficient and self-supporting as hunters and fishermen and craftsmen, or were employed in a few cases by the government: a people with modern transport, communication and living, who only some ten or fifteen years ago had leaped the gulf between the primitive, nomadic life of their forefathers and today's white welfare state society.

I was only just beginning to appreciate the magnitude of this leap and learn more of the people who had made it, when I reversed the order and left the civilized amenities of Pond to go out with a party of narwhal hunters, forsaking the kindergarten for a tent on the floe edge.

ॐ *Chapter 2* ॐ

The "floe edge" was always cropping up in conversations, and was beginning to assume almost as legendary a quality in my mind as the "unicorn of the sea," the narwhal itself.

Often I had watched the return of the hunters: the women, who had sometimes waited long hours on the shore, walking out over the ice, the excited children running on ahead to see what was lashed on to Atata's komatik, the soft laughter; then the unloading, and the family climbing the hill below my window, the grownups sometimes carrying a length of dark gray and white patterned skin, slung between them like a hammock; the children, unable to wait, already wielding expert knives to sever bite-sized pieces; the men's faces burned almost black from the sun.

The "floe edge" was, in fact, the barrier of ice gradually retreating before the open seas. At present it stretched across Baffin Bay from far beyond Button Point on Bylot Island to the northeastern tip of Baffin, about twelve or fifteen hours' journey away by skidoo. There the narwhal were beginning to congregate for the spring migration deep into the inland fjords of Milne Inlet, where the females would calve and they would remain until the autumn's first ice. They came down from the north, from wintering in polynyas, those permanently ice-free areas to be found even in Arctic waters, traveling together in small pods, following the Greenland halibut or polar cod shoals. Now the early arrivals would be cruising along close to the floe edge to avoid their enemies, the killer whale and Greenland shark, waiting for leads to open up in the ice — where their only other enemy waited for them with harpoon and gun.

When the full migration is on they have been recorded as passing a point on Bylot at the rate of about three hundred an hour. They are still fairly plentiful — a rough estimate of their number is about ten thousand in the Canadian-Greenland Arctic alone — and fortunately only the Eskimo may hunt them (even they were restricted to five in 1971). Soon, at the catastrophic rate of disappearance of the rest of the world's whales, they, and their small cousins the various porpoises, may be the only representatives of the family to be left for our descendants, so the more protection the better.

The solitary spiraling tusk has intrigued the imagination for centuries, being bound up inextricably with that of the mythical unicorn — as which it was sold to an unsuspecting public. A cup made from the horn was reputed to absorb poison, a useful vessel to have if you expected any of the Borgias to drop in for a drink in those days. The Vikings shipped the horns home as far back as the eleventh century, so the kings of Denmark acquired their famous "Unicorn Throne"; the Chinese traded for them with the Siberian Eskimos, using the ivory both for carving and for ingredients in potions; and even Elizabeth of England had one, brought back with Martin Frobisher, whose book *A True Discourse on the Late Voyages of the Discoverie* (published in 1578) showed the first picture of one properly implanted on the forehead of a "fish" and not on a four-footed animal; "We found a dead fishe floating, which had in his nose a horn streight and torquet, of length two yards lacking two ynches . . . we supposed it to be the sea unicorne. . . ." The picture is delightful: a very finny fish, with a large round head and human eyes, the lips curved back in an indulgent smile.

Despite the fact that narwhal have been known to us, at least in print, for centuries, remarkably little is known about their life cycle in factual detail, nor has anyone come up with a valid explanation of the horn's uses; even the more commonly accepted theory today that it is merely a sexual embellishment, like a cock's comb, does not hold too much water, as occasional females have been killed bearing a horn. Nothing is known of parturition, except that it occurs after the spring migration up the fjords; and there is only one report of a mating witnessed — by an Eskimo in Melville Sound — which was performed by the whales,

standing vertically in the water with their bellies turned towards each other. Unfortunately, I have no statement of the season. But in August the narwhal often has a foetus twenty–thirty cm. long, and when in June it comes back after the winter, the females generally have foetuses of about one-and-a-half m. A newly born calf has been seen in a flock of narwhals in June at the same time as a female with a foetus of about forty cm. was caught in the same flock. The narwhal is not supposed to have any definite breeding season.*

The dream of every Eskimo in areas of narwhal migration used to be to witness a savssat — when the returning stream of whales delayed too long and they were trapped by ice in the straits or fjords. There is a dramatic account of one of these that occurred in 1943, when hundreds of narwhal and white (beluga) whales were using a breathing space in the ice "No bigger than a Greenlander's house. . . . Side by side they emerged so close to each other that some of them would be lifted on the

---

* "Expedition Den Danske Thule og Ellesmere Land, 1939/41," in Christian Vibe, *Marine Mammals*.

backs of others and turned a somersault. . . . First rows of Narwhals, then White Whales, and then again Narwhals — each
species separately. It seethed, blobbed and splashed in the opening.
With a hollow, whistling sound they inhaled the air as if sucking
it in through long iron tubes."

There is no longer any survival exigency about the arrival of
the narwhal, no need to burn the blubber down for oil lamps,
cut the skin into thongs for dog traces, or remove the sinews for
sewing clothes. There remains a marketable curio value in the
ivory — a perfect ten-foot tusk in the cooperative shack in the
village was priced at $250 — but I do not think it is that which
sends man and boy into such a fervor of excitement. I think it is
the prospect of eating muktuk again, the sweet, nutty-tasting
skin, which is the supreme gastronomic delight to an Eskimo,
all part of a spring ritual. That, and the good old atavistic
urge to return in triumph from the hunting grounds — and of
all trophies, what more uniquely worthwhile than the white
tapering horn of the unicorn of the seas, so strange and beautiful, with its sinistral convolutions? And not forgetting the deep,
obvious delight of the Inuit in the long, long day of their now-
sunlit land.

I had longed to go with them, to camp out on this magical
floe edge too, to be where the action was, but did not know how
the idea of taking along a couple of strange female Kabloonahs
would appeal to the hunters. Families did occasionally accompany them, but essentially it seemed to be an all-male pastime.

But, "no sweat — no sweat at all," said John Scullion, when
we put it to him (as he was to say to any other problem put to
him during our stay, however trite or monumental), and within
a few hours he and Rick Hamburg had fixed everything. Rick
had many friends among the young men of the village, and
spent much of his spare time, winter and summer, on hunting or
fishing trips with them. One of these was Danielee, and it was

arranged that we should go ahead in a day or two with him and
five other Eskimos, traveling with three skidoos and komatiks.
Rick himself would be coming out later, and we'd see him
somewhere out there; just bring our sleeping bags, and enough
food for about ten days, for if all went well, on their return
they would leave us to camp out on Bylot Island, at Button
Point, picking us up again the following week.

We rolled up our sleeping bags, dropped some spare clothes
into a duffle bag, filled a wooden box with Pilot biscuits, dried
fruit, cheese and canned meat from the Hudson Bay store,
remembered the can opener, and decanted some morale-boost-
ing brandy into a plastic vinegar bottle. Each of us had a carrying pack that could always be got at en route, containing our
own individual whims. Susan, for example, finds it impossible
to live without a sketchbook at hand, at least four hunting
knives for sharpening pencils, and an endless supply of peppermints. I find that I can deal with almost any situation with a
knife with a screwdriver on it, a roll of adhesive tape and fruit
gums. In addition to these, this time, I had spare sunglasses,
mitts, and a heavy movie camera protected by foam rubber and
all its appurtenances. The only thing that filled me with alarm
and despondency about the days ahead was the thought of
operating that camera in these particular circumstances. I had
been used to a cassette-loading, compact affair, which could be
whipped out in an instant, but this was a beautiful Beaulieu
16mm, a professional job, electrically operated, and with all
sorts of dials, lenses and things to remember. I had already
practiced loading it in the kindergarten, threading the fiddly
film through gates and levers, and making the right-sized loops.
But the kindergarten, at a solid table, with warm hands, was one
thing. Clumsy frozen fingers, and the glare of sun on ice, was
another. The battery could not be left screwed into the handle
because the cold would exhaust it, so it had to live, along with

the spare, in the nearest pocket to my body. If we met anything interesting en route it would probably be gone by the time I assembled everything.

About 5 P.M. the following day, the men carried our gear down the hillside, and, bulky in our extra layers of clothes, we waddled after, to watch it lashed down on the komatiks, along with oil drums, guns, caribou skins, stoves, etc. There were three komatiks, one about twenty feet long and the other two about seventeen feet, a twenty-foot tow rope attaching each to its skidoo. I was to ride the large one, with Elizee, Danielee's brother, on the skidoo, and as the brakeman in front of me a small cheerful goblin called Jootah, who had a smile almost as wide as he was long.

Dogs pottered around, and were booted out of the way. Wives and children stood about and watched. John and his wife, Colly, came down to see us off. Then, with an ear-splitting revving of the engines, we were off, in single file, in a twisting path that threaded around the inshore ice cracks. For the first two or three miles I was rather unnerved: tense with the novelty of movement, I could not hang on to anything as both hands were clutched around the precious pack sack; and I was unable to sit sidesaddle as the Eskimos do. My legs were so much longer that they trailed on the ice where surface water gushed up my boots, while astride there was no anchorage for my heels. I longed for a prehensile tail.

(One realizes *why* the Eskimos have evolved into such a short-legged and compact people, after traveling with them for a while; height is nothing but an encumbrance in this land.)

Finally, I lashed the camera around my waist — if it went I was going too — and after a time became relaxed and in tune with the movement of the komatik, feeling the separation and coming together again of the cross slats (which are lashed to the runners with cord to allow for this), and hiking out in harmony with Jootah when the heavy sled swerved in too wide an arc from the skidoo. It reminded me of crewing in a dinghy. Jootah was a joy to be with, all four feet six inches of him: he was the "merry little fellow," the jolly elf of nursery tales to the life, in his all-in-one sic-a-doo suit, and a frame of furry dog hair around his pointed hood and round smiling face. He used the oil drum lashed to the front like a steering wheel, and over the rough ice was seldom still for a minute, sometimes running alongside as though starting a motorcycle, sometimes vaulting from one side to the other to control a tricky turn. When water sheeted up and soaked us, he thought it the funniest thing in the world, and laughed so much he nearly fell off, and this in turn made him almost double up.

From then on I was to find that everything dire was a joke — if a skidoo got stuck, or someone or something fell off, or a wrong route was picked — the more calamitous the situation the more side-splitting. I began to wonder what heights of hilarity we would reach if skidoo, komatik and all plunged through a seal hole.

Those first few miles close to shore were long and tortuous. The skidoos soon separated, each driver picking his own route, sometimes through water nearly a foot deep on the surface of the ice, sometimes skirting horrible, deep, black holes, or charging the narrower cracks. There was obviously quite a bit of navigational competition. Sometimes when the skidoo would get stuck on a crack, too wide to buck the runners over, Jootah would rush forward, and help frenziedly to manhandle the skidoo over the gap. Almost before the runners were down, the engine burst into life. Jootah would take up the slack on the tow rope, and as the great long curved runners of the komatik bridged the gap, he would leap aboard again, looking anxiously around to see how much ground we had lost. Once we miscalculated a shortcut and had to retrace, losing so much time that the other two teams looked like black dots, traveling north now, away from the shore. They had come to an open impassable lead and were running up its edge, looking for a narrowing. Elizee stopped at the lead and stood up on the skidoo seat, Jootah got onto the oil drum, and they surveyed the scene in silence. I stood on the food box and surveyed it too: to the right the broad blue lead curved into a nasty-looking maze of cracked icepans, and beyond that there seemed to be nothing but a stretch of open water to the shore. I would have plumped for the left-hand turn after the others, and without delay, but Elizee lit a cigarette and continued to contemplate the shifting ice. Suddenly he was down on his seat, the engine roared, and without a backward glance he was off. But I had been a passenger long enough now to know the form, and beat him to it with my crash dive for a handhold as the komatik jerked forward. Jootah, crouching like a monkey on the drum, looked around and we exchanged knowing, triumphant grins. We twisted round the evil-looking patch, and then I saw the reason for Elizee's urgency: an icepan on the far side had partially cracked and swung in on the offshore current, making a momentary bridge. Jootah seized a harpoon pole and ran ahead to probe. He nodded. Elizee went straight at it. I clutched the camera, shut my eyes — and we were over, running flat out over a wonderful expanse of free ice, Jootah crawling past me from the back of the komatik, where he had swung on at the last moment. By the time the others had found their way across and come back down the opposite side of the lead, we were well out in the front, and waving smugly.

I sat sideways now, relaxed and content, my back to the sun, and watched our long shadows fly over the ice as the Baffin shoreline passed by. Only the rocks and the beaches behind the built-up ice barricades were free of snow. Kuktiyuk beach went by, with two lone Eskimo houses, then the cliffs climbed and sank again to the snow-covered meadow with one derelict building that had been the original site of the Pond Inlet village. Beyond the sheer cliffs of Beloeil Island, Mount Herodier reared out of the ice, a black symmetrical cone towering over the narrow passage. I could see a wooden cross, lonely on the far shore, for here in the lee of Beloeil the deep water had been safe anchorage in the days of the whalers: Albert Harbor, a place where they could even winter safely if caught by early-forming ice. It was a sunless, cold place, gloomy and oppressive, with the sheer inhospitable cliffs, and I thought of the men who had spent the long months of darkness there, and wondered how they had kept their sanity. "A more desolate, bleak and forbidding spot than Albert Harbor can scarcely be imagined," wrote one of them, with what seemed to me today to be commendable understatement.

Something of them had lingered on in Pond, for only a few days before I had been in old Inoogah's house, and had persuaded him to play his concertina for the tape recorder, thinking that whatever came out would make a nice contrast for my Arctic Symphony. To my complete surprise, out from Inoogah's wheezy squeeze-box came reel after Scottish reel, played with such authentic verve that I could hardly keep my feet still. He said that he had learned them from his father, who in turn had listened to the whalers making merry.

Beyond Beloeil, huge boulders that had crashed down from the cliff bastions were scattered like black islands on the ice; little purple patches of saxifrage flowered bravely in barren cliff crevices, and the strata lines dipped and curved crazily from the first great stirring and pouring and heaving that made these mountains. Sometimes there were fascinating plateaux cut with geometrical precision; sometimes the gray mare's tails of newly released waterfalls; and glaciers, one nearly run out, the terminating ice some thirty or forty feet deep, black and melancholy, and somehow disturbing.

About two hours out we made the first of several stops for tea. Jootah had the stove unearthed and hissing in an instant within the shelter of a wooden box, a saucepan of snow on top, and by the time the others caught up, the tea leaves were in and being given a good boiling. Along with everyone else, I ladled in several spoonfuls of sugar, which normally I detest in tea, but which out here turned it into a heartening ambrosia, as the cold was now intense, and I'd long lost contact with my feet and hands. The Eskimos seldom offer tea or food, we had already found — if you don't help yourself it is assumed that you don't want it. We learned something else at the first tea stop: when they are ready to go they go. We were subconsciously in a sprint position most of the time; by the time our driver had one foot on his skidoo, his hand reaching for the starting cord, we'd have leaped like hares aboard the komatik, hanging on for dear life against the first great jerking backward movement.

And I learned out there to throw social inhibitions to the winds, for these stops were always made on ice so flat and endless that even a lady elf wouldn't have found an icicle large enough to retire behind. It was alright for the men: they just turned their backs in that immortal contemplating-the-horizon stance. At first I used to conciliate my environmental hangover by erecting an imaginary sign that said PUBLIC CONVENIENCE about thirty yards away, and head for it, dropping an imaginary coin into the slot on the imaginary door for good measure, then closing it behind me. Then, after a warning shout from one of the men who had noticed that my site was perilously near a seal hole or rotting ice, I moved in closer pretty rapidly — and soon after that shed my morally supporting sign forever, thereby saving myself a great deal of mental and physical exertion, to say nothing of the pennies.

We would be leaving the Baffin shore now, heading out into the open to cross the twenty odd miles that lay between us and the Bylot coast. This way we would skirt the piled-up blocks of broken ice that marked the end of the *Manhattan*'s attempt that spring to force a passage through to the east from the Alaskan oil fields. The huge U.S. tanker was especially built with reinforced bows for this purpose.

It grew colder and colder as we left the shelter of the land. Criss-crossing, weaving back and forth up the cracks, we took the full force of the wind shrieking down from Baffin Bay. I was wearing a string vest, flannel pajama jacket, heavy wool Guernsey, two light Fiberglas jackets, a down-lined hunting jacket with the game pockets down, and a long rubber smock over all — plus long underwear, thick trousers and pullover windproof trousers. But the wind still managed to sneak in. By the time we were halfway over I was almost paralyzed, even though I tried to keep up my circulation by heaving and pushing when we were stuck, and jumping up and down when the men went ahead to probe for rotten ice.

Now the skidoo was giving trouble, stalling and refusing to start after running through water, and there were endless sessions of upending it and tinkering with its innards, while all the time the wind howled and the Bylot shore loomed black and inhospitable, and never nearer. The men worked with bare hands, seemingly impervious, not laughing quite so much, but still cheerful. The other teams had long since drawn ahead and out of sight, so my heart leaped with relief every time the engine burst into life again. The tent was on Danielee's komatik, and it would have been a long, cold walk to Button Point.

Perhaps Jootah sensed that my morale was flagging a bit, for when we eventually reached the shore he pointed to a distant headland and said, "Bun Point, yes," and of course I brightened at once. He was a sound psychologist: thereafter every headland we rounded he would point to the next, "Bun Point, yes," and I, poor trusting innocent, would fall for it hour after hour. But at last, unbelieving, I could see the black dots of skidoos or boats lying below a low-level promontory, then three tiny tents perched above. About two miles away the skidoo broke down again. I left the men taking it to pieces, and set off for the distant point, following the tracks of a skidoo around the cracks.

It was hard going. There were two dog teams staked out on the rocks, so closely curled with their backs to the screaming wind, their heads thrust so deeply into paws and tails, that they barely acknowledged my passing: only a slit eye opened here and there. Three tiny tents, one just some plastic sheeting secured to a pole and weighted down with boulders, strained and billowed wildly. There was no sign of life; probably they were all asleep, but I didn't know which tent to insert myself into. Eventually a tent flap unwrapped an inch or two and I recognized the mitt that poked through. I crawled into a small, green, windless haven. There was just room for me to shut the flap and kneel on the threshold. Susan was crouched over a Coleman stove on the left, and Murta, the hunter, whose tent it was, had to stand bent over to make room for me. On the sleeping platform of skins beyond was Tabitha, his wife, feeding a tiny baby. A four-year-old boy, snugly wrapped in a cocoon of blankets, blinked sleepily beside her.

I was so paralyzed with cold I could barely manage to say Hello. But it didn't matter, for no one spoke anyway; there was only the hissing of the primus and the now-muted sound of the wind. I crouched there, unmoving, within a strange movement of light. The moment is frozen forever in recollection: the low sunshine outside the tent, the Coleman flames flickering across the thin, green walls that billowed and fluted in wonderful color-shot shapes to the buffeting of the wind, while against this background Tabitha sat like a small graven Madonna.

Eventually Murta went out. Tabitha laid the sleeping baby down, then, all without altering her position on the skins, she pumped up the stove, made some tea, hacked off some bannock with her round, razor-sharp ooloo, dabbed on some jam from a can, then picked up some crochet work and got on with it. Clearly her duties as a hostess were over. We emptied the tea leaves out of a couple of mugs, filled them up and reached over for the bannock, delicately removing the longer caribou hairs from the jam. Susan, her back pillowed by a bag of seal meat which felt curiously pneumatic, fell asleep. I took my boots off, and laid the insoles on top of the kettle; then kneeling there I slept for a while too. It had been a long day's night.

I always marveled at the Eskimos' indifference to the cold. Tabitha sat there, her legs in blue, woolen stockings stretched out before her, her tiny sealskin kamiks laid neatly at the bottom of the sleeping platform, wearing a cotton dress and a thin cardigan. The only other article of clothing I could see was her white, duck cloth, duffle-lined amouti. By comparison, we were grotesquely bulky, and not even faintly warm.

Jootah's expansive grin poked through the tent flap and indicated that we were off again. We thanked Tabitha and said good-bye in our best Eskimo, which sent her off into a fine fit of giggles, but whether from embarrassment or merriment, there was no way of telling.

The big komatik had been unloaded and a boat lashed on instead. Some caribou skins were thrown in, and we scrambled up to the impatient revving of the skidoo. The wind cut like a knife as we went flat out over the great expanse of frozen sea toward the floe edge, about ten miles on.

It was so exhilaratingly ludicrous, hurtling along in a boat,

high above the ice at 3:30 A.M. in brilliant sunshine, that I felt
quite slaphappy. The round heads of seals reared high on curious necks all round, plopping back into their breathing holes on
our approach. One, who was basking on the ice quite near,
seemed to have mislaid his hole, and flip-flopped to and fro in
obvious panic. But he was quite safe today; the men had their
rifles loaded and slung, but were not going to waste precious
time on seal meat when there was a prospect of muktuk. A flock
of murres came from nowhere, whishing overhead to wheel in
perfect flashing unison against the blueness of the sky, then
wheeling again to overtake us, heading as we were for the open
water. Far away to the north, huge, fantastically shaped icebergs glinted in the sun below the black-looking cliffs of Cape
Graham Moore. There, at Akpah, Elizee had told me, the murres
nested in their tens of thousands, and there, in a week or two, the
men from Pond would go to scale the cliffs for the highly prized
eggs.

The horizon stretched out, white and featureless for miles —
until suddenly I saw low flocks of birds skimming over shapes
that had not been there a moment before. Then, almost as suddenly, so deceptive are distances out here, the shapes reared
up into an endless procession of weird ice sculptures — and
there, in unbelievable contrast to the dazzling still solidity of
ice, was a great stretch of open water, blue-black, rippling
gently against the sheared-off floe. So this was the floe edge, this
most dramatic meeting of elements; no wonder men's eyes
brightened when they spoke of it, for it was breathtakingly
beautiful, a fairy-tale land filled with unexpected color. The
baby bergs drifting by sparkled in the sun, their icicles turned
to rainbow prisms, their captive colors ranging from palest green
and aqua to turquoise and deepest blue below the waterline.

There were scores of birds. In the brief stop, while the men
searched the water, I saw flocks of king eiders, old squaws,

murres and guillemots over the water; and there were gulls
everywhere: fulmars, kittiwakes, Icelandic, and many others
that I did not have time to identify then. I longed for the dese-
crating noise of the engines to be shut off, so that I could hear
what must have been the most wonderful clamor.

But we roared on, running along the water's edge for miles.
There were signs that others had traveled this ice highway too,
for as on any other highway, there was litter. However, here
the litter was more exotic: the skinned carcass of a seal, the
picked-clean rib frames of a whale, an abandoned skidoo windshield, a piece of torn track, and what I thought in the distance
was a twin-bladed propeller shaft but turned out to be the
recently hacked-off tail flukes of a narwhal.

At one point, Danielee, in the lead shouted and pointed:
"Quilalukan, quilalukan"; everyone screamed to a stop, grabbed
a gun and rushed up the ice like a team of Olympic gnomes —
they take short steps and cover the ground at amazing speed.
Halfway out in the channel, three glinting black backs curved
through the water, in close line astern of one another. Inevitably,
rifles cracked, even though the whales were far out of reach.
The men returned, laughing and chattering; the leading narwhal had had a fine long tusk, they said; and we zoomed on,
everyone ecstatic about what looked like a good omen for hunting prospects.

At last Danielee stopped at a place where the ice dropped off
abruptly in a sweeping curve, the baby bergs and piled-up ice
shapes massing on either side — a perfect open platform with
the advantage of ice height for better observation. The following
skidoos and komatiks pulled up in a semicircle, a blessed silence
descending as the engines were cut. Danielee undid the lashing
on a komatik and dropped off a dark blubber- and oil-stained
bundle. We would camp here, he announced. "*All* of us in that
one tent?" we said in dismal unbelief, as he started to lay out

something about six by eight feet on the uninviting ice. "Plenty room," said Danielee cozily.

We clambered out of the boat and stomped around, greenhorns, not yet knowing what to do or how to help. The six little figures (we seemed to have gathered an extra one at Button Point) scurried around; one crawled inside the tent, the others hauled and pulled; the canvas heaved, bulged and began to rise slowly into shape, until at last the grinning, furry-framed face of Jootah poked out triumphantly from the entrance flap. Suddenly we began to giggle helplessly — it was so like two aging Wendys watching the Lost Boys put up the little house in Never-Never Land: so unreal that any moment now Peter could come winging in with a harpoon in his hand. Jootah must have thought we were laughing at him, for, obligingly, he repeated his performance, appearing and disappearing at the tent flap like a Cheshire cat. By this time I had hiccups, and this the men found hilarious. We stood there, eight little dots around a tent in the middle of Baffin Bay, laughing as though the first joke had been told in the world.

It seems a trivial incident to report at such length. Yet it was to be quite momentous, although I did not realize this until much later, for from now on there was a subtle difference in our relationship with the Eskimos. Up to now it had been pleasant and polite enough, but with a curious, indefinably negative quality. Now an easy acceptance gradually flowered. To me, the Eskimos became individuals, some more appealing, some wittier, wiser or warmer, no longer a group of ethnic strangers behind a language barrier.

Perhaps the laughter released tension on our part; unless one is very young or supremely confident, there must always be unconscious tension in a new environment with strangers; one treads overwarily. Perhaps this was true on the part of the Eskimos too. Or, perhaps it was just simple relief to find at the end of fifteen hours traveling that the strange female Kabloonahs with whom they had been saddled were not going to be tiresome. Whatever it was, the difference was there, and was to infiltrate back to Pond eventually; and I have been thankful ever afterward that I was able to go on this trip within a week of first arriving, at the most impressionistic stage. There could be no way of life closer to the land, no more real contact with its people than against their own background; with no artificiality of a settlement, no other white advice, influence or interpretation. Just us, learning by ourselves, enjoying ourselves; *all* of us.

The men did not bother to hoist the tent up to its full height; being so uniformly small, they could stand erect inside the way it was. They laid the caribou skins out on a sleeping platform at the back, lit a Coleman, and threw the duffle bags in, going in and out with an easy stoop. Susan and I, both of average height, had to crawl in on our knees, and remain on them. (By the time we returned, we must have shuffled miles, and mine felt as though they had been to Mecca and back.) We crouched over the Coleman, thawing our hands, still given to sporadic hiccups, devouring like starving dogs the frigid, rockhard peanut butter and jam sandwiches cut so long and providentially ago in the kindergarten. We washed them down with a good restoring gulp from the vinegar bottle, and instantly felt overcome with sleep. Elizee appeared, yawned hugely, removed his boots, threw himself down on the skins, and was asleep in an instant. From the sounds outside, it sounded as though the rest of the men were off hunting, but I could not keep my eyes open long enough to look out, and followed Elizee's example. The caribou fur was incredibly soft and comfortable over the ice.

I woke briefly a few hours later to the strange sounds of a baby crying, and found myself squeezed against the tent wall like the outermost sardine in a can, for the tent was crammed with people — visiting Eskimos, and our own hunting party

returned, plus Rick and Mosesee. Framed by the sunlit, open flap
was a bloody hunk of narwhal meat on the ice. I tried to count
heads, but gave up when the numbers became humanly impossible and fell asleep again, only to waken almost immediately to
excited shouts outside. There was an instant mass eruption.
High on his observation post among the ice pinnacles by the
water's edge, Kaminah was silhouetted against the sky, his rifle
up. Cruising lazily past, momentarily framed between the small
bergs on either side of our ice stage, were four beluga whales:
beautiful white curves rising and sinking against the dark blue
of the water, so beautiful that I was guiltily glad that they were
out of range. Safe, too, was the fluid, black bulk of a walrus,
surveying the scene from a drifting ice pan.

"Aaaaa-oooo-aaaah," bellowed Danielee in imitation behind
me, so closely and unexpectedly that I must have leaped a foot.
"Ah, ah, ah-oooo-aah," he let forth again, trying to call it within
range, but this the walrus, with sad world-weary face and
drooping tusks, very properly ignored.

The boat was propped up on its side by an oar, and everyone
gathered in its shelter for a brew-up of tea and muktuk. The
vividly patterned strips of skin lay on the ice, smaller strips of
it being cut off, the technique then being to slice off at lip level
the portion protruding from the mouth. It looked so easy, but
after several near misses of my nose I gave up and ate less dan-
gerously. The inch-thick layer of gristlelike substance under the
skin was unexpectedly sweet and delicious, of a texture that
melted away in the mouth almost immediately.

Then the men loaded the boat on the komatik, three or four
of them clambered in, the rest jumped onto skidoos, and with a
roar of engines they were off to hunt far up the floe edge, where
the wind and tides had shifted the pack ice to form a narrow
channel. There the whales must come within rifle range, and
there, if the hunters were lucky, they could get the boat

launched and a harpoon in before the body sank. There was plenty of room on the boat, they indicated, and I was torn between longing to go and doubt that I had recovered the stamina yet to withstand possibly another fifteen hours' exposure to that wind, with no protection whatsoever. Common sense — or cowardice — prevailed. I'd shoot the narwhal they missed out there with my camera back here, I said. They took off, leaving us, it seemed, when the sounds of the engines had throbbed at last into silence, in sole possession of the Arctic.

A wonderful feeling of peace descended upon me — whether from the silence or because I had made the decision, I don't know. I speared the last piece of muktuk and sliced it off successfully, without thinking. The pressure was off. The world had stopped rushing by. There was time now, to stand and stare, to listen, to look around. Time, above all, that had no conventional meaning, so that one could eat, sleep and wake at the dictates of the body alone. I had tried to achieve such timelessness on two or three occasions in my life, but it had never been truly possible: either there was human intrusion with a watch on its wrist, or darkness fell inexorably to remind one that another day had ended. Only here, with the sun circling the sky, could one remain unknowing.

At that point, of course, I wondered what time it was. I never found out; for I took my watch off there and then without looking at it, and stowed it away in the pocket of my one clean shirt at the bottom of the duffel bag. I would not be needing either this trip.

Time now too to get to grips with the camera. I fetched it and wandered off down the floe edge. Susan was kneeling on a jacket on the ice before the dismembered head of a narwhal carcass, alternately blowing on her bare fingers and sketching. She seemed equally euphoric. The head was extraordinarily asymmetric, owing to the one-sided growth of the tusk, which is really a grossly exaggerated tooth. It had been removed, and it was possible to see the socket and surrounding bone structure. There was a large, ragged cavity of flesh missing right down to the bone on one cheek, and a smaller one high up on the other. So this must have been the one that Mosesee and his party had brought ashore, either mauled or bitten by a polar bear; and that was why the carcass, lying some distance away, its entrails in a rounded heap beside, had been left untouched except for the skinning; the wounds had gone septic and would taint the flesh. The tusk was lying on a komatik now, only about three feet long, its straight white spiral marred only by a ring of brown-red blood at the base from the extraction. Nearby lay a small seal, as yet untouched, its whiskers fanned out in a perfect ellipse on the ice, a frozen droplet at the end of each one. I turned it over — it felt curiously fluid, like a sack filled with mercury — and felt the rubbery flippers, astonished to find that the bone structure underneath was so like that of my own hands, the long claws taking the place of fingernails.

Like following a river, every bend around the floe edge was different; and each difference altered even as one watched, with ice pans parting and reforming or a phalanx of icebergs crowding in before the wind and tide one moment, only to be jostled out of place by another. Sometimes the movement was imperceptible, and then it was like walking past an endless exhibition of glistening abstract sculptures grouped around ice-blue grottoes, with here and there a view of the dark moving world beyond, through a translucent grill of pendant icicles.

There was a continuous background medley of sound, rising and falling in volume with the wind: a gentle, constant lap-lapping at the ice edge; creaking, crushing, whispering and whining, sometimes even a high-pitched hum like the wind in rigging; the cries of gulls and long-tailed jaegers overhead; the excited, rushing patter of a flock of a hundred guillemots' feet on the water; the high-pitched scream of terns; sometimes geese calling far out, snows and whitefronts, or the amazingly melodic gossip of old squaws drifting across the water.

There were always scores of dumpy murres criss-crossing the water, and, more occasionally, flocks of eiders, both king and common, or the handsome American scoters. And always the noisy, squabbling fulmars on the ice. Pure white Icelandic gulls drifted over, silent and ghostly, to me the most fascinating species of all the gulls out there, and one that I never tired of trying to film. There were glaucous, ivories, and kittiwakes too; and once only I saw a solitary sabine, the forked tail and sharp black contrast of the wing tips etched at the most beautiful angle against the sky.

All this life and activity dropped away immediately when I turned my back on it: the contrast was dramatic. At this angle, the farthermost northeastern tip of Baffin lay some sixty miles across the ice, the snow-covered mountains sweeping around until they disappeared over the horizon where, in a temperature inversion, they reappeared like a mirage of Manhattan skyscrapers. To the west lay the straits we had crossed, with the towering triangular shape of Mount Herodier spectacular in the distance, and to the east the Bylot range with its fleet of icebergs riding across the horizon. Yet, as far as the eye could see, in all this limitless expanse of icebound land, except for the slowly moving masses of cumulus, or the occasional bobbing of a seal, there was no movement. I felt suddenly overcome with the magnitude of it all compared with the infinitesimal dot that was me standing in the middle of a frozen sea; so infinitesimal that it seemed ludicrous that anything so nearly invisible could have cold hands or feel hungry — could do anything in fact except just *be* and no more. I have seldom felt so utterly content.

I was often to experience this most peaceful acceptance of my microscopic unimportance. I think I began to understand then how this land binds so strongly, and is bound up with, its people. The two are one.

But if I shrank out there, there was one part of me that didn't — my shadow. I delighted in this new shadow — always so long and different, never leaving me, night or day. When it went before me I was continually amazed that it belonged to me, and when it followed I would sometimes turn my head quickly to make sure that it really was there.

Time passed on the floe edge like a dream. There was always something to watch or do around the tent if I was not off wandering, stalking seals, or perched on an ice platform somewhere, trying to film birds. Men came back from hunting, drank tea and ate muktuk, or bannock fished out of a potato bag, then fell asleep; while others might roar off up the endless white road, rifles slung across their backs, to scout the farthermost ends of the floes. One never knew who one was going to wake up beside in the tent. I might creep in and insinuate my sleeping bag into the row, only to wake up and find myself gazing into an entirely different face. Once, woken up by the barrage of snores, I meanly photographed my bed companions, lying like Oriental mummies in a row, Susan flanked cozily in the middle. The result should interest her grandchildren one day. Another time, when I had come back from taping the sounds of birds and moving ice at the water's edge, I found everyone asleep. Jootah was stretched out on a skidoo, his feet sticking out by the windshield, snoring gently, his face still wearing a beatific smile; Kaminah, bundled up in his sleeping bag, was flat out on a komatik, only his dark glasses and the top of his hood showing, his snore of the basso profundo class. Inside the tent was a mixed chorus of tenors and baritones. I stole around, taping all for posterity. When I eventually played back my symphony at the end of the trip, the men went into gales of laughter, playing a kind of "guess who or what" game.

More usually there was someone on watch. Once I found Mosesee at the edge of the ice with a harpoon gun, waiting for fulmars to come in for the bait he had thrown out on the end of a line, looking like any stone carving one has ever seen of a hunter, in his fur-trimmed parka and kamiks; still as a carving too, patient, somehow conforming exactly with this landscape. He hit one and it dropped to the water, one wing stretching out to its full extent, straining to take off again; but in vain, for the other wing hung broken and useless, pierced by the barb, the white feathers stained in a spreading red. It stopped struggling, and paddled captive at the end of the line, the eyes round and calm and uncomprehending. Mosesee pulled the line in, tugged the barb out, then threw the bird back into the water. It fluttered and struggled there, keeled over, then drifted slowly down wind, caught up by a small chunk of ice, its eyes still alive and watchful, looking toward me it seemed, so that I looked away and would not look back. Half an hour later, I picked it out of the water a hundred yards away, spread the unbloodied wing on the ice, and marveled at its structure. Then I took a pinion feather so that I would not forget it. There were others shot that day, or night, and left wounded, but that was the only one I cared about.

Kaminah woke up and took turns with Mosesee. Later they used a rifle, but without much success. Some of the rifles were something to behold with awe and astonishment: .303s of considerable vintage, one with the magazine secured to the barrel with a cord. When the fulmars became too wary for further sport, Kaminah planted an empty cigarette packet on the ice and everyone took turns throwing the bladeless harpoon at it. They were like little boys playing — but playing with toys of a once-necessary skill; like the little boys playing below my windows at Pond with dog whips and bows and arrows and miniature harpoons. By the same primitive token, there was no conception of cruelty toward the wounded fulmars.

This group of men had grown up together at Mittimatiluk, as they called Pond, and had always hunted together. They were very much the "in" group of the community, most of them with steady incomes from administration jobs, and therefore not dependent for their living on hunting and fishing like the other able-bodied men. I had heard one white person in Pond dismiss their activities as "holiday hunters" only. But I thought this disparagement misplaced: to sneer at what we ourselves have brought about by territorial annexation and "progress" seemed unnecessary; to me they were the best and most hopeful kind of anachronism in a land of anachronisms. I had met enough apathetic Indians similarly caught up in a "betwixt-and-between" emergence into a welfare state world, who had abandoned their old skills and involvement with the land forever to exist on government handouts, to rejoice in what I found here.

They were young men, yet had been brought up in the days when all men were hunters and Pond but a huddle of shacks and tents around the RCMP and Hudson Bay post, living in family groups up and down the coast. Danielee and Elizee, in fact, had been brought up in the family band of one of the most respected, and later famous, hunters of all, Idlouk, who was their uncle.* When the boys' parents had died, they had been adopted by their grandparents. There is frequent mention of them in Douglas Wilkinson's *Land of the Long Day*, for Idlouk

---

* I heard the next year that Idlouk, by now famous, and more and more involved with the Kabloonah way of life after a film had been made of his life, became an alcoholic, and met his death as a direct result — his sled going over a cliff in a white-out, when he was incapable of recognizing the danger. The endearing and wise Kidlak, his wife, also drowned her bewilderment at the transition in the bottle.

was Wilkinson's Eskimo "father," and he lived within the group for a year. One reads of Danielee and Elizee as boys, driving the dog teams, hunting with their elders in a real, hard life. They could — and still did in winter — build an igloo. Today they lived in heated houses, rode skidoos, and collected their wage packets regularly. Who is to evaluate the difference?

The amount of English that they spoke — or wanted to speak — varied from Jootah, who knew only a few words apparently, to Elizee, who was not only completely fluent, but was also something of a specialized interpreter, for he had worked with the controversial Gagnier on the new concept of a standard pronunciation in written or syllabic Eskimo. They were, as were all the Eskimos we were to meet later, very helpful and patient in correcting our pronunciation as we daily struggled to add more words to our vocabulary.

I do not know what they thought of us — if they thought at all, which I doubt, so happily absorbed were they with their own activities. Yet it is extremely unlikely that they had ever met anything like us: strange white women, old enough to be their mothers, without any apparent commitment to a particular project, do not come winging into Pond for a protracted stay every day of the week. Or, if they ever had met such phenomena, they would certainly never have been thrown so closely into their company. But they took us completely in their stride, showing the most refreshing unconcern for our well-being or years. Most refreshing to us, straight from the word-wasting officiousness and nannydom of white society, was the assumption that if we were out there at all we must be capable of taking care of ourselves. We were left to our own devices, with no crash courses on how to recognize rotten ice or avoid snow blindness; no dire warnings about wandering too far, meeting polar bears or falling off the ice floe; no nagging organization about where to perch or when to go with a komatik or looking back to see if one is actually on or not — if not, it is assumed that you don't want to be, and good-bye. I had noticed that children were treated by their families in much the same way at Pond: no one ever explained or warned, or laid down the law, no one ever said Agah — "no," — to children: children learned by observation and experience what was out of step within a family group. The children at Pond were the most happy, self-contained and naturally courteous little people that I have ever met. I remember seeing a tiny girl run out of a doorway, half naked and barefooted, and into the snow. Her mother stood in the doorway and watched; her father smiled indulgently; neither said anything. Of course the little girl fell, got to her cold little feet again, and, weeping bitterly, returned to be laughed over and led inside again. There was not a word spoken, but I felt quite sure that that would be the last time the child made that mistake. (White opinion varied as to the wisdom of such upbringing: the majority were in wholehearted admiration of the end-product, and if they had children of their own tried to apply the same general principles; one or two diehards condemned such fecklessness.)

Similarly I gave up stalking seals with my camera after one boot went through some seemingly hard ice and water gushed over its top. The resulting discomfort was enough. Anyway, the seals outwitted me every time.

Only once did I hear the word No. The projecting forward skids of the skidoo were caught under a ledge of ice, and Mosesee, the smallest of all, was hauling it backward out of a watery trough. I was moving down to the limit of my boot tops to try and free a skid, when he suddenly shouted, "Agah, agah!!" and grabbed my jacket; just ahead of the skid, at the end of the gentle incline of submerged ice in the trough, was a nasty round blackness, a seal breathing hole, just like some supersized bath outlet, into which I would undoubtedly have slithered. "Ha, ha, ha," said Mosesee, and "Ha, ha, ha," I agreed penitently. After that no one scoured the depths of watery expanses more thoroughly than I. I could think of nothing more humiliating than being fished out of a bath outlet.

I went out with the men to hunt farther up the floe edge only on the last day, knowing that this would ensure that they did not stay out an indefinite and unbearably cold time. Because it would be the last time, the expedition had something of a high-spirited holiday air about it. We climbed into the boat and headed off west, along the wide, glaring ice road winding for sixty miles across the bay to the mountains.

The other skidoos were ahead, tow-free this time; and for a while, as they really gunned it and we followed flat out, the boat swaying like mad, I felt just as though I were out on a weekend meet with the local chapter of Hell's Angels. It changed to a Wild West thriller when Elizee, who had Jootah riding pillion, maneuvered his machine until the skids were an inch away from our komatik runners; then Jootah leaped, with all the aplomb of one galloping Apache onto the horse of another, into the bow of the boat.

They slowed down at last to run watchfully along the edge of the open water, and eventually we stopped where the channel had been closed off by shifting floes and icebergs, forming into a peaceful lake of almost Mediterranean blue, so still that the clouds and ice sculptures ringing it were mirrored perfectly.

There were long rafts of murres out in the middle, king eiders, and occasional ivory gulls and kittiwakes overhead. The men settled down to smoke and watch, but I could hear enticing little noises in the distance, so took my packsack with the camera and walked on about half a mile to where I could see little black figures congregated on the shore ice of the newly formed lake. They turned out to be guillemots. Lost in the joys of courtship, they were so unheeding of me that they let me come within a few yards before plumping indignantly into the water. There were more than a hundred of them, many in pairs, the male displaying; others were strung out in lines of three or four playing a kind of follow-the-leader game, where all turned with well-drilled precision when the leader turned.

The wind had dropped away completely; the sun struck so warmly on my back that I took off my jacket and knelt on it in the cover of a friendly little iceberg offering a perfect ledge to support the camera. I could afford to be a bit more extravagant with film footage, for it was obvious that there could be no chance of a narwhal hunt now — we would have to go miles to find open water. The atavistic half of me regretted this, not to be able to record the noises, the excitement, even the actual kill if possible, and to watch my companions in some real action. But the other half was entirely satisfied, content merely to be there among the mundane little guillemots, in the warmth of the sun. I taped their rather uninspired courting noises instead, and filmed their choreography. Besides, by the time the men returned to pick us up at Button Point next week, there would be many more narwhal arrived, and I would be considerably more adept at switching lenses on the camera.

But there was to be no Button Point that year, for on the way back Danielee heard from a party of other hunters that the ice conditions had changed so much that Murta and his family, and those in the other two tents we had seen, had already left. There could be no question of leaving us there by ourselves (had we been of the stuff that even contemplated such intrepid isolation — sixty transportless miles from the nearest human being), as the uncertainty of the ice now could delay the men's return to the floe edge next week.

This was a blow — not just because we had looked forward so much to exploring the archaeological possibilities of the point, but because we did not want to leave this close association with

the land yet; we were not yet ready to return to roofs and people, or reminders of time.

Then Danielee came up with a splendid compromise: they
would drop us off with the tent at Kuktiyuk instead, beyond
Herodier, where two Eskimo families lived. There would be no
difficulty in coming back to pick us up on that side of the coast.
So we settled for that.

We were at least heading into the sun a good deal of the time
on the return journey, which made it seem a little warmer; but
the difference in the ice since we last crossed this stretch was
very evident; cracks had widened to impassable gaps, and we
had to cross and recross the strait to find a passage. Sometimes
the ice looked like a vast lake with surface water over a foot
deep in places, and lying treacherously over holes and cracks.
Once I despised the skidoo for a noisy abomination, but this
trip I came to have the greatest admiration for it. In this terrain,
these extremes of weather, it is like a toy — or a sports car
doing the work of a tractor — and its sturdily adequate big
brother has yet to be developed. The cost of its upkeep in the
Arctic is tremendous, and I think only the Eskimos, superb
natural mechanics and improvisers, could keep skidoos running
in these conditions. We could not skirt the terrible broken wake
of the U.S.S. *Manhattan* this time; great slabs and hills of ice
knifed through and cast down, to be flung up again at random
by the pressure of the ice pack into nightmarish white moon
mountains. Here the Eskimos showed how they could handle
these little machines, and I marveled at the beating the seemingly frail skids and narrow treads could take. The men rode
them like jockeys, sometimes kneeling, then rising in the saddle
and gunning them so that the machines literally jumped seemingly impossible gaps. Then up the crest of a cast-up slab of ice
and down into the valley, the komatik behind coming down
with such a sickening thud that sometimes I felt as though every

bone in my body must be shaken loose; bucking the next ridge, then across great open ice lakes, the water up to the foot rests, and foaming out in a magnificent spraying wake.

Jootah was soaked, his stocky little body keeping me comparatively dry as I hung on to the rope lashings for dear life. Every time we came down with an extra hard thud he would turn round with an ear-splitting grin. Thudding up and down behind him like a bag of scrambled bones and brains I reminded myself that I was out here being battered and jolted and soaked for my own pleasure, that I belonged to no order that insisted I do such a thing — so I dutifully bared my own teeth in masochistic joy.

We crashed, thudded, swayed and groaned our way out of the *Manhattan*'s Badlands until at last we came down on the flat — the greatest expanse of open water yet. I thought Mosesee in the lead would surely have to turn aside from this, but, no, we went straight at it, the skidoo transformed into a motorboat, the wake pluming out and the water hissing through the cross slats of the komatik. By anchoring my feet under the lashing, I was able to balance enough to get the camera out, and, greatly daring, film as we boated across the ice. Jootah turned and pointed back, nearly falling off, he was laughing so hard: Danielee's skidoo had given up in the middle of the lake, and was half submerged; the komatik was floating free, Susan perched high at one end while Kaminah poled with a harpoon from the other, over the rippling, sunlit water, for all the world as though they were bound for some idyllic summer picnic in a punt.

After the others had undoubled themselves, they grabbed for their cameras too (every Eskimo has a camera under his parka it seems), then waded out to tow the skidoo onto a small raft of ice above water level. Tea was brewed, and there followed another paralyzing wait while the engine was restored to life.

We could not have picked a colder place, for we were right in the middle of the strait, the wind sweeping down with nothing to break it between us and Baffin Bay. Mosesee, so small that he must have been nearly up to his waist in water, sat beside me, wringing out his socks and trousers, his feet navy blue with cold. For the first time I saw a cold Eskimo. I gave him the spare socks covering the camera lenses, but he must have been frozen for the rest of the trip.

Hours later, we ran through the dark, sunless fjord between Beloeil Island and the mainland, then out into the sunlight and the more gentle sloping shores beyond Mount Herodier, heading tortuously inshore now for Kuktiyuk.

Someone said it was about four o'clock when they deposited us on the beach there with the tent, a Coleman stove, and two pots encrusted with seal stew. Bunnee, who lived at the other end of the beach, would put the tent up for us, they said, throwing down three soaking caribou skins as an afterthought. Then they hurried back across the ice to the skidoos. I had thought they meant four o'clock in the afternoon, but it turned out to be morning.

We stood there in the brilliant sunshine, warmth seeping up from the sand, hungry, exhausted, but possibly the most satisfied travelers in the Arctic — it was such sheer heaven just to be standing still on terra firma, without every muscle straining against the next thud. My sleeping bag must have traveled most of the way under water, and was useless; however, there was plenty of driftwood, so we soon had a fire going and the caribou skins steaming in front of it as well. On the hillside behind, the snow ended in a long drift, and we picked a site beside a fast-running little stream emerging from it, about fifty feet before the frozen sea.

Two figures appeared at the far end of the half-mile beach — Bunnee and Sangoya of the second house, apparently not in the least surprised to find a couple of Kabloonah female castaways needing a tent put up. Presently three or four children arrived too. We had not had a meal for about fifteen hours and were ravenous, but the pots looked as though they could only be cleaned with a mallet and chisel; when Bunnee saw me extemporizing with a knife he pointed back to his house, and indicated that his wife would do a better job, so I set off with the pots. Inside the small immaculate oven of a room was Kownah, with a thin bony face, a delightful smile, and in the back of her swallow-tailed amouti a large baby. There was a heavenly smell from a pot on the stove, and I wondered what rare Eskimo delicacy she was cooking at this time of the morning: when she lifted the lid it turned out to be popcorn.

We were thankful we were not in the isolation of Button Point when it came to lighting the stove, for we found that we had forgotten everything we ever knew between us about Colemans; either it sulked dimly and went out, or else it flared alarmingly, until Bunnee suddenly appeared, as though summoned by telepathy, and quelled it with masterful adjustments. We had just cooked some rice and opened a can of ham in the lee of the caribou skins when he came staggering back over the beach with a spring mattress, of all unlikely things, on his back, much of its insides bulging out from the coils, and of a strange and dubious color — but a mattress, a heavenly, dry, hip-receiving mattress nevertheless. He put it in the tent, smiled shyly at our profuse thanks, and departed. This was true Eskimo hospitality. We had decided to take turns on it, tossing a stone for the first, and were sitting on the sand, forks poised hungrily for the first stab into the rice, when we saw another mattress approaching in the distance, apparently propelled by two little sealskin-booted feet. It passed us sideways, trundling along unswervingly, looking blankly over our heads while we viewed it as stolidly in turn, beyond surprise, then lowered itself to a horizontal position and entered the tent. We decided it must be looking for its mate, and got on with the rice. A minute later a little man we had never seen before emerged from the tent, smiled deprecatingly, and scurried back across the sands.

We thought that we had better turn in immediately before we woke up to find that the two spring mattresses now lying tidily on either side of our tent on the middle of an Arctic beach had been as dreamlike and unreal as the fact that we were sitting there at all, eating dinner at six o'clock in the morning. It was all very strange. Out on the ice beyond us a tiny gnomelike figure, its face fur-ringed under a pointed hood, was now riding the rear half of a tricycle around a small iceberg, which didn't help.

We retired. The sun made shadow pictures on the tent walls, so that a pair of mitts drying on the peak and a pair of socks farther down on the wall looked exactly as though someone were climbing over. A bee, bulky and huge in its Arctic coat, appeared and disappeared like a furry tennis ball being batted back and forth against the wall beside me. I fell asleep.

The days passed at Kuktiyuk even more timelessly; eating and sleeping whenever we individually felt like it, although we usually managed to coincide over the stove for one main meal. These were strange and wonderful concoctions, consisting basically of instant soup, into which anything to hand was emptied. Any personal addition too bizarre for the other's taste, such as strawberry jam with tuna fish, could always be evened out with curry powder. One of my better midday snacks was one of the ubiquitous, awful, tasteless Pilot biscuits thickly spread with honey, then topped with sandy garlic sausage and cheese. Once we feasted on puffballs — something I had never expected to find on northern Baffin — and for salad there was always plenty of tart, refreshing, mountain sorrel.

Far removed from the area where the dog teams had been staked out during the winter, our end of the beach was clean, fine sand, newly washed by the retreating ice. But the far end, before the two dwelling places, would have made even Hercules pale before its Augean awfulness, with the winter's debris revealed in all its thawing horror, the garbage piled on the ice waiting to drift out to sea. I never knew which was best at first: to hack on blindly over the carpet of blubber, hairs, seal meat, dogs' muck, etc., without looking down; or to pick my way as delicately as Agag. Susan, who traversed it frequently in pursuit of models, had mapped out a trail for herself, and was moderately unmoved, but I couldn't stomach it in the end, and took to the long way round by the hillside. Sangoya's dog team was staked out on the far bank of a rushing river beyond, blending in all their variegations of markings and color against the heap of glacial boulders there. Nine of them howled, slept, yawned, and stretched there at the end of their chains, but the tenth lay dead, half in and half out of the water. A team was useless at this particular stage of the ice, with so much water lying on the surface, but in another week they would come into their own again, when Sangoya would load his boat onto a komatik, and everybody, including the dogs, jump in as well to cross the open water.

We used to amuse ourselves from time to time with compiling a *Gentlewoman's Guide to Travel in the Arctic*, and one of Susan's more inspired contributions one day was How to Remove Blubber and Other Noxious Substances from the Boots: as far as I remember, the Gentlewoman requested a Friendly Native to fashion her a long scraper from some indigenous source such as a walrus tusk or a caribou bone, "the scraper end of which could be amusingly fashioned in the shape of a hand, and would later furnish the traveler with a nostalgic memento of this harsh land . . ." Pending this, we used to wade down our creek to the tent, dragging our boots in the gravel to clean them, but even this did not work.

I wandered over the hills much of the time, in search of wild flowers and birds; sometimes over a carpet of the little cream bells of Arctic heather, or saxifrage, purple and white, with here and there the brilliant yellow splashes of newly opened poppies and Arctic buttercup, palest greens, grays and gaudy oranges of lichens. Sometimes I crossed snowdrifts lying deeply in the ravines, or squelched through bogs ringed with Arctic willow, the catkins soft and gray as a baby seal, but mostly it was over deep hummocky moss or on the smooth rocks of the cliffs runing back from the headland at the entrance to the bay — it was from this same vantage point that Dr. Mansfield, the Canadian authority on narwhals, once watched more than two thousand pass by below. Once, stretched out there, my head pillowed on the heather, I slept in the sun, and waking, thought for a moment that I was back on my own West Highland hills, and could have sworn that I heard sheep bleating. It was only when I looked down and saw the ice far below instead of the Atlantic that I fully awoke.

I saw various plovers, including the semipalmated and the blackbellied, so close and unafraid that I was able to photograph them, ptarmigan and snow buntings, and once two sandhill cranes flapping across the horizon toward Herodier. But, apart from the ever-present Lapland longspurs, there were few birds yet.

We became very friendly with the Eskimo families, our vocabularies enlarging daily under their tuition, although I could not take much more than ten minutes inside the houses, as the temperature seemed to range around 90 degrees, and tried to time my visits when something was going on outside, such as Sangoya's wife doing the washing in a tub, or Kownah scrubbing a sealskin, the baby sleeping all through her energetic movements, although sometimes it was nearly upside down. Or perhaps Bunnee would be sitting on his old skidoo seat by the river with a chunk of soapstone on the ground before him. When I first saw him he was making the preliminary cuts, with a saw, then an ax, then later a file. He worked on it all day, with long frequent pauses while he just looked at it, or, when it was small enough, held it between his hands and considered it. Gradually the outline took shape — a polar bear, nanook — until one evening he walked across the beach with it, finished, polished to a deep dark-veined green. Another time he brought a little ookpik, the young snowy owl. He was an accomplished carver, and later we saw one of his larger pieces, with curving shapes of narwhals interrelating with the rounder walrus below, so that the group was poised on a triangle of a pair of walrus tusks and a single twisting narwhal tusk. He polished with a constant buffing of hands, or a piece of duffle.

Sometimes the little boy, Ahmoos, came and watched us, or followed around silently, apparently fascinated by everything we did. I don't know when he or the other children slept, for it seemed that any time I looked around there would be his small figure trundling over the ice on his half tricycle, or poling himself on a raft of boards and jerry cans up and down the small, stinking lake that had formed below his home with the runoff from the hillside. The two little girls played hide-and-seek indefinitely just offshore where the pressure ice had formed all kinds of wonderful caves and crannies. Once Kaminah and a fourteen-year-old boy came to see how we were getting along, and stayed for a meal. Another time three skidoos appeared, halted for a while offshore, bound for some Centennial fun with a traditional seal hunt — using only the old methods with harpoon and line. Sangoya presently appeared with his harpoon, loaded up his komatik and joined them. I watched them out on the ice beyond our tent, the skidoos drawn up in a ring, gallons of tea being washed down, and everyone fooling around — all boys together, out for the day, with the school principal Brintnell easily distinguishable, towering over everyone else; then they set off across the strait to Bylot, leaving us to our nice primitive peace and stillness once more: only the sounds of the river roaring down from the ice field, the cry of hunting jaegers on the hillside, and the little groans of shifting ice.

The sun beat down, twenty-four hours a day, and we were lucky, for on the night that Mosesee and Kaminah set out from Pond to pick us up, the clouds were massing and the barometer dropping.

We left the mattresses lying side by side on the beach, and looking back on them from my perch on the komatik, against that background of ice, snow and hill, they looked pleasantly idiotic and surrealistic. It was a wet ride back, and we arrived off the point in the long, mellow sunshine of evening to find a wide open expanse of water, green hills, and the people wandering around in a relaxed summer mood. There was so much open water that we had to leave the skidoos quite far offshore, then use the komatik to bridge the gaps while we sat on board and were towed over. I was on the back, kneeling; it was very slippery where seal meat had been cut up, and when the komatik suddenly reared in one place, down I went inexorably, holding my precious camera aloft as I went, so well conditioned by the trip that I remembered to say Ha, ha, ha as I went — fortunately only up to my waist. But instead of joining in the laughter this time, Kaminah and Mosesee clucked such nice and unexpected concern as they pulled me up, stood me on my feet, and plucked vile debris off my parka, that I cannot believe it was only the camera they were concerned about — even though Mosesee did have it out of its bag in a flash to examine it.

The kindergarten was warm and welcoming, even the tiny chairs amazing luxury to sit on, and the bath, of course, Paradise. It was reassuring, too, to read all those nicely printed cards again, stating so clearly that WALLS were walls, or DOORS doors, so that one still did not have to think for oneself. No more sand and caribou hairs in everything we ate, and no more limitations of one mug, one place — and no more utter peace and solitude. If Pond once had seemed like the end of the northern world, now it seemed like a tiny metropolis. For a while I felt exhausted — not physically, but mentally, as though my mind and vision had been exposed to too much; perhaps I had been overdiminished by the magnitude of it all, and needed an interim for some regrowth.

❧ Chapter 3 ❧

It was a wonderful time for regrowth. Spring had swept the snow from the land, leaving traces of color everywhere; now summer was painting them into vivid life. It seemed that even as one watched, flowers unfolded. Where there had been only an anticipation of green in the morning, by afternoon there was a bright covering. The bare hillside below the window was like a rock garden now, with busy little lemmings running through the saxifrage and poppies, and longspurs nesting too trustingly near the round depressions at the end of the bank that marked the sites of ancient dwelling places. They were called Thule houses and could have been anything from eight or nine centuries old, when the first wave of the Thule people, from whom all present Eskimos are descended, spread across the eastern Arctic. Sitting within the rim of the nearest one, photographing the longspurs, I prodded around the walls, and was rewarded with a flint harpoon head, beautifully pressure-flaked.

I spent hours up on the hills, picking sorrel with the women, in search of wild flowers, or filming a pair of golden plovers whose nest I had found almost as they were putting the finishing touches to it. Sometimes I skirted the cliff edge until I came to the height of land that commanded a view for miles down the strait. It has obviously been a lookout since time immemorial for there was a well-defined path winding around the heather and rocks. Often I would find someone up there with a telescope, and one week when a hunter and his family were overdue someone was there almost all the time. (An official air search, or Atlas Aviation diverting from their usual "sked run" course, would only be called in if someone was exceptionally overdue; most delays in returning meant that the hunter had been forced off the ice to camp on Bylot or farther down the coast until such time as conditions changed, or he had mended his skidoo or komatik.) When the cold drove me back, I took my field glasses to my window, where there was more than ever going on — more birds arriving daily, children playing, women sitting for hours with telescopes watching for the first sight of their men returning. Sometimes, now that the pack ice was shifting to and fro, it would take almost half a day before the distant black dots materialized into a dog team or skidoo, and the path through a maze of cracks and open water was found at last. Far across on Bylot the snow traced gullies and crevices down the mountains, spread across the blackness like great white antlers.

There was much more life to be seen in the village too, with the children out of school. As I walked through the village, practically every small child capable of speaking said Hello — the only English word that most of the preschool children knew. I had made friends with three little boys aged about six or seven, Jootanee, Joshua and his brother Levi. If I sat outside on the rocks they would come running to join me, taking turns with the field glasses, or looking through the long-distance lens of the camera and telling me what was going on, like a running commentary on some sporting event — one evening it was Jootanee's Atata out in his boat, and every time his rifle cracked I would be informed of the results. There was never any anxiety about the fate of the camera or glasses in their small, brown, competent hands. Sometimes they tumbled around with each other like puppies, but always my belongings were handed back to me first, and they never disputed over whose turn it should be with anything. In return they gave me a turn with their toys, obviously knocked together very rapidly by Atata or an elder brother, but even so, knocked together with a beautiful ingenuity: a seal rib for a bow's curve, and a piece of tightly braided string, the arrow sliced from a piece of packing case; a tiny komatik, with the cross slats just nailed on, but with the curved runner ends neatly and accurately carved; a stick with a length of sealskin bound to it for a dog whip; a driftwood boat. Only once or twice did I see children playing with a ball — then it was some boys who had an old baseball bat. The first time I had a turn with the bow and arrows, the first arrow, by some fluke never before achieved, sailed for a creditable distance through the air, putting my stock up considerably. They retrieved the arrow and handed it to me again, but I was cunning and didn't risk a failure. My efforts with the dog whip had them almost rolling on the ground with giggles. One day Levi had a handkerchief-sized parachute with a small stone at the end of the strings, which dropped quite nicely and slowly for a few feet if you threw it far enough up, and I was allowed my turn with this too. In size they came up to my waist, but in throwing power we seemed to be shamefully equal. Sometimes they came along to help look for flowers and grasses too. They made the most endearing, friendly little trio; I particularly appreciated them when, strung out like a team of willing elves before me, holding hands, they would pull me up the last part of the hill when I pretended it was too steep for me, or carried the heavy camera. They were wonderfully patient language teachers too, repeating a word indefinitely until I said it to their satisfaction.

One could really have sat like an eagle in its eyrie, never leaving the kindergarten, and known all that was going on among the people, both Inuit and Kabloonah, for sooner or later they all came visiting. There seemed to be a completely free and easy relationship between all concerned, an intermingling, and, particularly on the part of many of the white people, a true affection and respect. Pond, I gathered however, had something of a unique ambience in the eastern Arctic, and postings there were very much sought after. There was a general policy of phasing out entirely white administration — a policy ideal in theory, but which in practice has lamed many an aboriginal council in its attempts to keep up with the speed of change today. But the Pond Inlet people seemed to be trotting along very comfortably, sound in wind and limb, and taking in their stride the changes that came about even during the two-year span of my acquaintance (they took over, for example, the post office, the telephone exchange, the Transient Center, and the water and sanitation contract).

I think this unique atmosphere at Pond came about partly because it was so far removed geographically from the somewhat dubious fringe benefits of civilization — most important of all, at the risk of sounding Pollyanna-ish, from easy access to alcohol (the cost of beer or liquor freighted in up there had its own sobering effect), and because its people could still live off the land. And partly because of the attitude of the white people, who, counting it a privilege to be there, gave of their best — not only to the people, but among themselves.

Of those who lived here all the year round each, whether teacher, nurse, game warden, RCMP or administrator, had seemingly developed a safe and (outwardly, anyway) peace-preserving attitude toward his fellows. One very, very seldom heard any criticism of personalities, but only He/She is so nice, does so much, is wonderful at. Occasionally, because one's an-

tennae were more acutely tuned through being an outsider, one
was conscious of tension between certain individuals, but this
was rare. I gathered that they had it all worked out during the
six months of twenty-four-hour darkness, when there might rea-
sonably be some stress within a small confined community. Activities, such as bridge, over which people in cities can tend to
become rather maniac sometimes, were recognized as potential
troublemakers and avoided, and anything involving competition. A good, safe activity, capable of being shared, arousing no
jealousy or competition, was photography: practically everyone
was madly interested in this, and many did their own developing, printing, etc. I had never seen such an impressive array of
Hasselblads, Pentaxes, Leicas, etc., as I had up there.

Another factor contributing to harmony was the average age,
which was around thirty or under: an age exposed to today's
precepts of "doing your own thing" and "make love not war" —
precepts very much in line with the outlook of the Inuit, who
have always been a nonaggressive people. It is also an age
uninfluenced by that difficult climacteric period, universally
shared elsewhere by those who have made it to the positions of
authority, during which strife is commonplace and mayhem
(verbal or otherwise) frequent. There was no rat race either; no
Keeping Up with the Joneses, as all housing, furniture, etc. was
standard government issue; and no constant noise — which I
sometimes feel could well be one of the heaviest contributing
factors to a lot of today's neuroses. Finally, and possibly most
important of all, it seemed that very few people there did not
acknowledge that it was not a question of one-sided instruction,
but that they themselves had much to learn from the Eskimos.

There was a lot of communal activity going on now too, particularly the first year, with all the extra Canadian Centennial
Celebration activities, such as the seal hunt off Kuktiyuk, and
the Spring Games organized by the council. These included dog

whip contests, when the contestants had to move two very small objects on the snow with the tip of the thirty- to forty-foot lash, skidoo races, and dog team races, with one of the latter for Kabloonahs only (John Scullion and Pat King, the Mountie, tied for first place). In one dog team race the women had to catch a man first, then tie him up after maneuvering him onto a komatik, and finally drive off on the course — this being a take-off on the occasional male practice of kidnapping a pretty girl and riding off into the sunset with her.

I saw slides of the community Christmas dinner in the school hall. Two long carpets of wide, brown paper had been unrolled on either side of the floor; on one side were laid roast caribou, seal, fish and other cooked goodies; the other side had the same, but uncooked. Everyone brought his own knife or ooloo, and sat on the floor, where, as John Scullion said, they ate themselves silly, Kabloonahs included.

One evening there was a community seal eat-out on the rocky headland just beyond us. It could not have been a more perfect setting, looking down to Eclipse Sound one way and up toward Herodier the other, nor more colorful, from the poppies and saxifrage underfoot to the blue and white of ice and water, sky and billowing cumulus clouds; and the people themselves in their brilliant blue or scarlet stockings, brightly braided white amoutis, and embroidered kamiks. Everyone was there, from grandparents to babies in hoods, and children running everywhere with bits of seal meat speared from a washtub in their hands. Only one thing set this picnic apart from any other village outing that I had known, and that was the peaceful quiet: children might be running around, but there was never any shouting or even raised voices. There was plenty of laughter, but even that was quiet.

Another evening I went to the movies — the last thing I had expected to do in the Arctic — in the school auditorium next

door. It was the *Looking Glass War*, a cloak-and-dagger episode
in color from John Le Carré's book, and complicated enough to
follow in terms of world-weariness, cynicism and cold-blooded-
ness, even when one had been exposed to that sort of thing.
Heaven knows what the Eskimos, the majority of whom had
never left Pond's immediate surroundings, can have made of it.
In fact, I thought halfway through, what impression could they
have got of the white man's behavior in his own surroundings
from any of the movies they saw? We must seem like people
from another planet, greedy, violent, lustful, promiscuous people too. The closeups in this particular example were all of the
Fraught-with-Meaning type, so that if one misinterpreted one
Fraught it was twice as hard with the next. Little children wandered around or slept throughout it — one lying like a flopped-
out puppy across the entrance threshold, so that everyone had
to step over him. Ootovah's teen-age daughter came in halfway
through with a squalling, hungry, baby brother in her amouti;
she divested herself of both and handed them over to her
mother. Ootovah, still with her eyes glued to the screen (where
a lissome brunette in a bikini was about to be bedded, with
much panting from the quasi-hero), stripped off down to the
waist, then hauled the amouti over her head for modesty's sake
and shoved the baby down the front. The yells turned abruptly
to a noisy glug-glug-glug — so close and loud beside me that it
outdid the pantings on the screen, making the hero sound as
though he were saying glug-glug-glug as he pursued the bikini.

I left when a truck driver, who had very decently given a
ride to the hero, had a knife stuck in his belly for his trouble
and was rolling around in death agonies, at the same time as
there were some pretty Fraught zoomings-in on the knifer's face
and white-knuckled hands. It was the second time in my life
that I have left a film because I was disgusted: not at the bedroom scenes (at which everyone had laughed indulgently) but

at too much cold-blooded, utterly callous violence. This time the disgust was intensified by my surroundings, and a hopeless dismay that the undiscriminating vision of the people here could be offered such a sick sample of how the other half lived, and of their seemingly brutish standards.

Soolah had told me that the people themselves did not like the usual choice of rooting, tooting gun-toting Westerns shown once a week, and thought the continual, and apparently acceptable, violence in them bad for children. But apparently there was no choice in the matter; the films came from Frobisher Bay, and were chosen there from personal white tastes. In another context, John had also told me that when he, or any of the other residents, went on leave no one would believe that he was not returning to some magnificent Hollywood-style home, complete with swimming pool, with a saloon of the Cheese Gulch type, everyone in ten-gallon hats and spurs, just down the road.

It was a time too to go fishing. Long thick strips of Arctic char (salmon trout) were hanging on racks outside many houses, the flesh a wonderful deep red. Sometimes we would come back and find that someone had left a two- or three-pounder in the kindergarten for us, and raw or cooked it was delicious. The run was just starting, the char going up Janes Creek and Salmon River to spawn.

The river lay about two miles west of the village, at the end of a long, curving beach. I first went there on a magical warm day when the shores and land basked in the sun, but the ice off-shore was shrouded in low mist. I walked through it, picking a route on the hard ice along the floes and around little captive icebergs and buildups of pressure ice. The colors out there were delicate and strange, enhanced by the mist through which the sun's shape appeared only as a soft diaphanous light. Here and there fascinating little pools had formed in the ice, each framing in its crystal-ringed depth a perfect composition of gently undulating fronds and leaves and streamers, aquatic plants and seaweeds in every possible color from yellows and ocher to vivid green and scarlet.

Other times I was to come via the long curve of beach, covered with white bleached bones and shells, usually forsaking it halfway to skirt the stench of two decaying Greenland sharks, and taking to the hill slopes, where Baird's sandpipers and snow buntings nested. Or sometimes I came over the hills from the village, past the two little graveyards, Protestant and Catholic, on the headland, where Arctic poppies flamed among the low wooden grave markers and a tapestry of blue willowherb lay stretched up the gravelly cliff, climbing up and down the gullies and ravines until they sloped down at last to the river.

It was a fascinating place, with an atmosphere all its own, filled with the sounds of the river, a fresh gentle wind blowing across the sand dunes, and always some shelter to be found within the hollowed circles of the ancient dwellings. An indefinable light of cheerfulness lay everywhere, as though something of the happy spontaneity of the days of festival and dancing still lingered. The cheerfulness was in no way dispelled by the two wooden grave markers, one a tall cross, the other a board, that dominated the beach approach; the graves lay one behind the other on the path through the sand dunes so that one always had to skirt them to get to the river. HECTOR PITCH-FORTH was carved on one, R. JANES OF NEWFOUNDLAND on the other. Mr. Janes looked as though he were pushing up through the sod, disturbing his covering boulders, but Mr. Pitchforth seemed pretty secure under his load of sand. No one seemed very clear who he was, apart from being a trader, but everyone knew about Janes, for he had been something of a cause célèbre. He had been murdered fifty years ago by an Eskimo named Nokudlo. Nokudlo had been elected to the deed by a group of Eskimos, who had decided that Janes, a trader, was a thoroughly bad character. The result was that Pond Inlet retains a certain fame as the most northerly site on which a full-scale trial has ever been held.

I was curious about Janes and Pitchforth, and eventually was able to investigate their lives further. (Their story is told in Chapter Six.) In the meantime, it was intriguing to discover that Nokudlo's wife was the Atagootsiak who had made my soapstone dolls — our Lily's grandmother. I do not know where Nokudlo was buried (presumably the RCMP, who had brought him to justice and were the sole authority in those days, thought that it wouldn't be quite the thing to bury him next to his victim), for the two little graveyards at the top of the hill beyond Pond were not in use until the coming of the missionaries, the Anglican church being the first established in 1928.

In the ecclesiastical settlement of the Arctic, whoever arrived first at a village gathered the majority of inhabitants into his particular missionary fold, this status quo having endured until the present times, conversion being rare. (Reading accounts of these early interdenominational stakes, one has an irreverent picture sometimes of the respective fur-clad clerics urging on their dog teams across some pagan white wilderness, rival banners — Anglican Mother's Union and Catholic Women's Guild? — flying on bravely, neck and neck sometimes as they sped toward the distant goal of some unenlightened igloo.) Thereafter there appears to have been no rivalry, however, but a high degree of mutual respect and ecumenism.

Pond was a good example, as Muqtar and his family were the only Catholics there, but Father Mary was probably the most loved and respected man in the whole community. His real name was Guy Mary-Rousselière, the Mary part being a family surname, not an Anglicization of Marie, but over the years of living first among the northern Indians and then the Eskimos he had become Father Mary — much simpler to say. Not only had

he contributed many learned papers on Arctic archaeology, but
he had written the most complete book yet on Eskimo string
games, those endless varieties of cat's cradle still to be found in
primitive societies throughout the world. Apropos of these, it
was quite amusing that I had given the Canada Council, as my
second reason for wanting to go to the Arctic, the desire "to
study Eskimo string games," not then knowing that any work
had been done on them — one of the first people I met was
Father Mary, author of an inch-and-a-half-thick book! After
thirty years of living among the Eskimo, mainly in the Pelly Bay
region, there was little he did not know about them. I used to
enjoy it when he came to the kindergarten sometimes — very
tall, very thin and aesthetic, still with a pronounced French
accent. He would sit perched on one of the tiny chairs — and I
would have liked to pick his brains indefinitely concerning some
of the information I had read or heard, for I felt that his was the
most balanced and objective opinion to be found.

His small flock just fitted comfortably into the ten-by-ten-foot
chapel leading off the living quarters of the white clapboard
mission. There was a calm and stillness in that tiny place,
austere, yet warm and colorful with the red flickering of the
sanctuary light, and the huge Arctic mural which he had
painted many years ago, an Eskimo scene with igloos, mountains and a frozen sea. It was a part of his house, yet completely
apart. There were always all sorts of fascinating things lying
around on his porch or in the living room: curved whalebone
komatik runners, stones, bones and artifacts; and in one of the
storerooms a huge arch of baleen, the stiff flexible substance
that lines the jawbone of toothless whales and acts as a kind of
sieve for plankton, krill, etc. It was about ten feet high, curving
down to a point in an ellipse from about ten inches wide, with
fronds of something like fibrous hair hanging from the inner
ellipse.

The Anglican church, only a hundred yards or so away, was a wooden building equally plain, dignified and in keeping with the land; the interior was plain too, yet somehow more impersonal, having no extras other than yellow curtains at the windows, and some beautiful inset work sewn into the sealskin kneelers. There were sturdy, well-worn wooden benches, a plain unadorned table as altar, and a long sealskin runner down the aisle.

The first year I was there Annakudlip's wife died, and I attended the funeral service in this church. Howard Bracewell, the minister, was away building a new church at Grise Fjord, so the service was conducted by Piteolak, the catechist. The church was crammed. I sat wedged in at the back, and was puzzled at first when every now and then a small child was held up high in the air above the heads of the congregation: at first I thought they were being held up for a better look, which seemed rather blatantly insensitive — then I realized that they were being slipped into the back pouch of their mothers' amoutis, their feet feeling for the hood entrance. It was the most relaxed yet devout congregation; children wandered quietly in and out of the open door; babies cried and were put to the breast to silence them; and there seemed to be a constant gentle murmuring, like the muted humming of bees, throughout the service. This, of course, was conducted entirely in the Eskimo language, and followed in prayer or hymn books printed in syllabic characters. Everyone sang full-throatedly and my neighbor, a large jolly-looking woman called Atagootiak, smiled encouragingly at me and pointed out the place in the prayer book, but I could not have read syllabics at that speed even if I had known what the words were, and could only join in with the recognizable Twenty-third Psalm. There was no overt grief, but Annakudlip's normally cheerful face looked pinched and gray.

When it was over, they put the little plain box on a stretcher outside the church, and the congregation wended its slow way over the river and up the steep path at the knife edge of the hill. Looking up from below it was an unforgettable sight, the whole colorful procession silhouetted in a single file frieze against a brilliant blue sky. Not wishing to seem intrusive I did not follow to the graveside, where a close semicircle now stood before Piteolak, their backs to the wind blowing off the frozen sea below, so that their heads conformed with those of the Arctic poppies at their feet, the slender stems all bowed before the wind.

The next time I went to church, the following year, it was a very different occasion: the wedding of Tabitha and Simonee. Tabitha was the daughter of Mary Alloolah, a most talented carver. Simonee came from Arctic Bay.

The bride was costumed in white lace, mini length, and carried a handbag; the bride's mother chose for her attirement flame chiffon, with contrasting emerald green woolen hose; the groom was attired in a brown suit and stiff white collar and tie; the Reverend Howard Bracewell performed the nuptial ceremony . . . etc. . . . etc. . . .

And the guests came as they were, babies, children, teen-agers, parents, packing the church so that Piteolak — a cheerful, widely grinning Piteolak this time — who was ushering more and more people into the already tightly jammed benches, had to seat the last comers sideways down the aisle — making progress up it for the bride and her father rather a tight squeeze, as they had to pick their way in single file around the children sitting on the floor.

I sat next to Elizabee, who had a tiny baby in her amouti, and two toddlers, one of whom fell asleep peacefully sucking on a bottle under the bench at my feet. Completely composed throughout, Elizabee somehow managed to keep one eye on her children while the other remained fixed devoutly on her prayer book. Even when it became very apparent as we knelt together that all was not fragrantly in order with the baby, now on her lap, she dealt with everything in the same unhurried way: fishing a diaper out of a bag as her lips followed the Lord's Prayer and unpinning the baby at the same time, she apparently decided that the catastrophe would be better taken care of outside. She stepped neatly over me and the sleeping child, not missing the Amen, and was back in midvoice by the second verse of the hymn that followed.

There was a great strong confident volume of sound in the singing, almost lifting the roof off. During Howard's prayers there was, occasionally, silence, terminated only by the soft murmuring response of adult voices. But for the rest of the time, as at the funeral there was a constant background effect of babies and of small children in motion: a murmuration of whimpers, whispers and satisfied burblings.

After Tabitha and Simonee had been officially pronounced man and wife, they immediately separated to sit one on either side of the aisle as before. The congregation sat too, while Howard settled behind the sealskin lectern cloth to give a good twenty-minute address — stirring stuff, if one were able to judge from the almost evangelical delivery and the unfidgeting attention of the adults.

After the service he stood at the door, shaking hands with everyone, babies and children included; then we followed the bridal party down the hill to the rectory, where they were to sign the register and have a cup of tea, while the rest of the congregation gathered in a cheerful chatting group outside the church, then slowly rambled back along the village road, or, in single file, up the hillside and over the airstrip to the far end.

We handed out mugs of tea to the bridal party, who sat stiffly around the sitting room. Outside the windows, a few

yards across the sandy beach, boat-length slices of ice went by
on a current, gliding as swiftly as if they were propelled by an
invisible engine, over water which was as blue as the Mediterranean, or as the little flat blue mats of sandwort scattered along
the shore. The three little Bracewells and their Eskimo friends
played together at the water's edge among small broken-off
bergs. Outside a nearby pen, a pale-eyed malamute husky
glowered triumphantly at her gluttonous roly-poly family of six,
captive within, two of them with her ghostly pale eyes, all yip-
ping their protest at being weaned, clawing at the wire of the
pen. In a few weeks they were all going to Resolute Bay to
replace the team of an old Eskimo there, whose own dogs had
been allowed to starve to death while he was in the hospital.

The wedding party did not stay long, and we left shortly
afterward, for Howard and Mavis Bracewell, in what seemed
like an endlessly busy parochial day, were already in another
aspect of it. They were going back to England soon, and were
arranging a weekly Sunday service — complete with hymns and
Howard's sermon, all on tape — for the months that the church
would be without a minister. When I looked back it was curiously like some Victorian rectory scene: Timothy Kudlo, a
hunter, square and bulky in his anorak, white duffle trousers
tucked into his sealskin boots, stood by the window singing a
hymn in Eskimo, while with one hand Mavis picked out the
tune on a little harmonium — they were trying out the Eskimo
words against the English hymnal, Howard taping the result.

The church played a large part in the life of Pond. The turn-
out for services was almost maximum, and weekday events, such
as young people's meetings, were also fully attended. It was
common practice among the older generation to take their Bibles
along even on a hunting or fishing trip. There was a very Scottish Sabbath flavor to Sunday — no children playing on the
swings, no noise of outboard engine or rifle shots across the ice

— and everyone wore their best, dresses for the women, and suits for some of the men, or their best duffle trousers and parkas. The men looked rather strange at first, as they all carried handbags — mostly women's ones, but sometimes the black business executive type — with their hymnals and prayer books inside. I used to enjoy watching them to-ing and fro-ing in a long straggling procession past the back window of the kindergarten. The services were of a good Victorian length, one and a half hours at least. Unknown to them, I even filmed the procession from there with a 150mm lens, a wonderful continuous reel of faces coming toward me: Ootovah and her family, Sam and Martha from the post office, Annagutsia, Jako, Nonatee, Oodlateetah, Blind Loetia (she had cataracts at age fifty-seven), Lame Martha — and all the other gentle-voiced smiling people I had come to know.

Prior to the coming of the missionaries, the "spiritual leadership" was in the hands of the Angakkoq, or Sorcerers, who were principally powers for good, such as bringing good hunting, curing disease, calming the weather. They seemed to have much in common with the Medewewin, the shamans of the Ojibwa and Cree Indians. But, although I have often felt that the veneer of Christianity lay fairly lightly over paganism among some of these closest neighbors in the north, and though there is no doubt that the occasional shaman still dispenses his wares among them — albeit furtively — there seemed no evidence of this in Pond. The last known Angakoot or sorcerer who seems to have done a bit of practice on the side was Lame Martha's husband: "Small Lame Martha," I had first noted in my journal,

who looks a bit like a cross between a witch and a vampire, with her two solitary upper fangs and long broomstick cane, was a model this afternoon. She says she broke her hip at Button Point, aged four, and didn't receive any treatment. She is the Martha who carved two of the figures I bought; she is also Inooga's daughter, and mother of Akoela.

Akoela was an interesting boy, a fourteen-year-old who had won a drawing competition, and who often came to borrow charcoal and paper, then sit totally absorbed at one of the kindergarten tables. About this time I had been trying to get information on how to play the Bones-in-a-Bag game; I had the little sealskin drawstring bag, filled with all the finger bones and knuckles from a seal flipper, but most of the younger women I had asked had forgotten the names of half the bones, and part of the essential layout. I had just returned from Kaango and Attagotik's one day, a couple of the "old type" who usually lived a long way down the coast, where Kaango had played the game with me, but he spoke no English whatsoever, and I was still totally confused about the characters. Akoela was there, drawing one of his friends. I laid the bones out on the table, trying to remember the form. Presently Akoela came over, watched in silence, then, still without a word, rearranged all the bones. I asked him to explain, and received a patient, perfect lesson: these bones made the igloo, these the sleeping platform, here were the two families on the platform, mother, father and child, and the seal to the right of the entrance door bones. Outside were two komatiks on either side of the entrance, and five dogs to each. There was also grandmother, and the thumb-knuckle chair into which she so neatly fitted. The bones were all put into the bag and given a good shuffle; then each player had a piece of string or sinew with a slip knot at one end which he dropped inside and fished around, hoping to withdraw a catch on the noose. The object of the game was to amass the greatest number of essential bones for the completion of the igloo.

Slightly surprised that my information had come from a schoolboy, it became clearer later on learning that he was the son of Lame Martha and her one-time sorcerer husband — he had come from a home where traditions persisted longer. His brother, Sam, was reported to be somewhat fey, with a habit of going outside at night, and shouting as one possessed to the spirits or to Jesusee. His father was unable to save himself by his own medicine, for he died of a complete stoppage of the intestine, but it is at least remarkable that he continued to live far longer than the normally swift end following such an untreated condition. Howard Bracewell told me that once when someone else was after Martha he did some "walking around the tent" (to restore her to her senses) and Martha was his again.

There was also in premissionary days a parallel to the beliefs of northern Indians in according spirit forms to animals. The animals themselves were courteously compliant about being hunted, so long as it was clearly understood that Man took no more than his needs for survival. This being so, it was a suitable return gesture to show some appreciation after killing an animal; seals, for example, being given a token dash of fresh water — something they did not often get in life, and therefore greatly appreciated. The Swedish anthropologist who told me this said that the practice was still carried out, although surreptitiously, today. I am a bit skeptical about this, though, unless the action were carried out more in the reaction of hidebound superstition — like throwing spilled salt over one's shoulder "in the devil's eye." (I certainly did not ever see this happen.) But possibly such residual superstition could also account for the fact that alone among animals the seal and caribou, both formerly so vital to Eskimo existence, are never never allowed to suffer more than is absolutely necessary in their killing: if a caribou is not killed instantly with the rifle, its spinal column is severed as quickly as possible with a knife.

I watched a group of adults and children one day, thoroughly amused by a cat playing with a live lemming. When eventually the lemming lay limp, a small boy produced another from a box for the cat's — and the general — amusement.

John Scullion had taken puppies away from families on occasion when the children had abused them beyond (his) tolerance, something no parent would do: if they had considered the puppy valuable enough, they would have taken pains to see that it was not available for torture. Seals, however, were a different matter: sometimes, if a baby seal were caught, the hunter might tie a rope to it and drop it back into the hole to lure the mother out from the cavern below the ice; then an accompanying child might be given such a baby seal to hold for a moment — they are the most endearing little things — but the child would never be allowed to hurt it.

I found it easier to agree with the anthropologist's observation about the emergence of the older people into present conditions of life: far from being like the northern Indians, many of whom so bitterly resent the breakup of the pattern of family life that they will go to all lengths to keep their young people from leaving the band, the older people here did not want to hold their young people back. Often they would not even tell them the old tales and beliefs, with the result that interested youngsters came to a white anthropologist to hear them.

It is mainly the Kabloonahs who, from experience of what civilization can mean, regret the passing of the old ways. But occasionally there is mutual response, as in Pond, when some of the parents and older people became enthusiastic over a school project that was a sincere and practical Kabloonah attempt to bridge the time gap. In this project, making sealskin kamiks, the boys of the upper grades were required to hunt the seals and make the frames on which to stretch the skins, while the girls were to scrape, clean and soften the skins, and eventually turn them into kamiks. (Only one of them had scraped a skin before;

only two had made kamiks at home.) The plan being outlined by the teachers, various mothers and grandmothers said they would come to the school to instruct the girls, and fathers and other relatives agreed to accompany the boys out hunting.

An interesting impasse then ensued: all were quite adamant that they should be paid for these services. Somewhat taken aback, the teachers suggested that as it was to be an extra-curricular home-town activity in which the children would be taught skills that they should have learned at home anyway, surely the parents would give their services free? Not a bit of it, said the parents firmly, you brought this situation about with compulsory education: no pay, no teaching of ancient skills. So in some cases the paradoxical situation arose of a father being paid the going rate for the hire of dog team or skidoo and komatik in order to take his son out hunting, or a mother receiving so much an hour for instructing her daughter's class in the making of kamiks which she, the daughter, had seen her mother make a hundred times at home.

Much the same situation (but this one revealing a far deeper gulf in ethnic understanding) arose over a project to cook mid-day school dinners during the bitter, dark winter months, when the teachers were concerned that many children arrived inadequately fed, either because hunting or trapping failures meant no immediate supply of food in the house, or for the more mundane reason that the adults were still asleep when the child left for school. There were surplus government stores available, and the idea was that volunteer parents should concoct a good nourishing meal from them — free. It was entirely a local idea and had nothing to do with the Schools Board. Again there was great enthusiasm — until the question of payment for cooking hours came up. But the meals will be *free*, said the exasperated would-be donors, conditioned from birth in a soci-

ety of volunteers; they will be for the good of *your* children, and
one less meal out of *your* pockets. . . . Surely filthy lucre does
not enter into such a scheme?

But, no cash, no dice . . . no meals, said the mothers with
firm indifference. They were paid.

What would have happened if their bluff had been called, I
asked, and the scheme dropped? They would have shrugged
equally convincingly, I was told, and said, "Okay by us then,
no meals. . . ." And it was explained that it would not have
been bluff, for that was not in any way part of the Eskimo
makeup; they simply meant what they said, and would have
been genuinely unconcerned had the meals not materialized —
unconcerned at marginal hunger in their children at any time,
and certainly not bitter or resentful if there had been any question of withdrawal of the scheme. It was left to the inexplicable
Kabloonahs to feel their usual burden of responsibility. (However, the Kabloonah worms turned, with a united refusal on the
part of the teachers, over the curfew idea. This was a wonderfully backhanded plan presented by the parents: if the teachers
were so insistent on teen-agers attending school, then they
should instigate a curfew system, and furthermore be responsible for seeing that it was enforced — all teen-agers rounded up
and returned home by 9 P.M. so that they could get sufficient
sleep to enable them to wake up in time and attend school.)

I was both amused and delighted to hear of this essentially
pragmatic and shrewd outlook — one that should stand the Eskimo in good stead in today's world — but most white people
involved felt baffled by such a mercenary display. George
Swinton, in his book *Eskimo Sculpture*, has this very pertinent
observation to make:

It is mostly in regard to motivation that Eskimo culture purists get
particularly upset. They decry the Eskimo's changing way of life and
everything that goes with it. They are unwilling to appreciate the Es-

kimo's unbelievably matter-of-fact powers of adjustment to the incredibly fast pace of cultural evolution from the stone age to a money economy, mechanization, and rapid transportation, all within a single generation. They are equally unwilling to recognise the Eskimo's need for changing attitudes and motivations in his life and art during this process of acculturation. How can they fail to accept, and even admire, the Eskimo's resourcefulness and healthy opportunism in reacting to these changes! No doubt, these changes are destroying the Eskimo's indigenous culture, but they are also improving the tragic conditions of his life and are preferable to the purist's romantic illusions.*

These remarks follow in context Mr. Swinton's point that it is time people stopped bemoaning the transition from the traditional or primitive to contemporary Eskimo carvings and started criticizing these modern works with an eye to appreciating the intrinsic artistic values of the truly inspired Eskimo carver for what they are, against no ethnological background; or at least trying to separate the pleasingly primitive and relatively uninfluenced works from those of the merely untalented aspirers. It is a worn-out cliché to say that things aren't what they used to be, just because Eskimos no longer carve for their own pleasure, but for bad old profit, and that furthermore they carve with an eye to what the white man understands and wants. Why should it offend the purists that they show the same business acumen over this skill as did the parents of Pond over the sealskin project? And if there are good, bad or indifferent carvers, surely it is up to the buyer to exercise his own discrimination and individual taste as in any global art market.

There will always be a market for garden gnome or birdbath sculpture, for excellent reproductions of Michelangelo or museum treasures, just as there will always be the buyer who recognizes for himself some stunning truth of greatness in an as

---

* George Swinton, *Eskimo Sculpture* (McClelland and Stewart, 1965).

yet unknown creator — if not always for himself, as a potential in the art dealer's future.

Fortunately for the general public, and fortunately for the Eskimo carver too, not only does his work nowadays represent an economic betterment of life, but he loves to carve — and the ability is inherent in him generally; thus there are less tasteless perpetrations available on the market than there would be if a like number of Kabloonahs had jumped on the art bandwagon.

It may be a generalization to state that Eskimos have an inherent artistic ability, but I think that few will dispute its validity when measured against a white criterion. Never was I more aware of this than when looking at the crayon pictures pinned up around the walls of the kindergarten. There were four non-Eskimo children represented there, and one could easily pick their pictures out across the room without looking at the names, for they totally lacked the strength, the homing-in on the subject, of even the least inspired of the Eskimo children's. Yet the subjects were commonplace enough to both ethnic groups, if not fundamentally at least visually, everyday things to be seen round Pond — school, children, dogs, komatiks, etc. There were two or three particularly outstanding children, and one little boy, Malachai, seemed uniquely talented. Where the average four- or five-year-old will draw a figure face on, or at most sideways, this child drew them every way: three-quarter face, or walking away with the head half-turned, looking up; if he drew the inevitable amouti-clad figure with a baby's head peering out beside the mother's, the bulge of the child's body hung heavy, not just the usual cut-off disc of a face. It must have been in the family, for his sister's work was of the same caliber, and I was told that their father was one of Pond's best carvers. It will be interesting to see what they produce later.

I wondered if this single-mindedness in creation, this absorption in form and subject divorced from the uncertain lines and distracting extras of the average kindergarten artist elsewhere, could have anything to do with the huge uncluttered Arctic landscape, so often unrelieved white, over which a relatively small number of subjects moved: there would be no visual distraction as in the south.

The difference between traditional and contemporary carving is not so much that the former was executed for pleasure, and more often in ivory or bone, and the latter for sale in soapstone, but that in the old days people carved *things*, not episodes or events. They carved something to be held in the hand that could be passed around, their concepts of bear, walrus, man or woman, or whatever they felt must emerge from the imprisoning stone. It was only when the white man, with his conceptual vision, suggested that they carve scenes from hunting or domestic life, that they complied, producing the explanatory figures of today — men harpooning seals, women skinning foxes, lighting lamps, etc.

This contemporary carving style fits in harmoniously with our classic occidental approach to art, but is foreign to the old traditions of the north. The ancient Eskimo lacked such artistic "refinements" because they did not fulfill any need. The Eskimos did not need to be reminded of such day to day episodes, nor were they tangible.*

There is an amusing account of the results of an immediate transition from traditional to contemporary at the instigation of a white man in Rasmussen's Fifth Thule Expedition.† Rasmussen had asked an Eskimo named Au to draw the four walruses on an ice floe that he had just described as drifting by his

---

* George Swinton, *Eskimo Sculpture* (McClelland and Stewart, 1965).

† *The Report of the Fifth Thule Expedition, 1921–24*, under Knud Rasmussen (Copenhagen: Flyndalske Boghaindeln, 1928). Vol. VI, *Material Culture of the Iglulik Eskimo*, part A, p. 104.

home. But Au found paper and pencil so difficult that he went off to get his carving knife and a piece of ivory instead. Several months later he produced the result: "Male walrus and three females drifting on an ice-floe, while Au watches them from land through a telescope, with his wife and daughters seated beside him."

(Soon after reading that, I read a news item in the Sheffield *Star* that reminded me irresistibly of Au's carving: "A 36-year-old man wearing a skin-diving suit was seen emerging from a pond at Tapton Golf Club with 435 golf balls, it was stated at Chesterfield yesterday.")

Entirely for my own objective occidental pleasure, one day I asked Piteolak to carve me a lemming. He is not one of the great carvers whose works will increase in value over the years, but it always seemed to me that there was something of the quality of the man himself in his carvings, as though he had a real affection for his subjects — grave, dignified snowy owls, seal pup, all with huge trusting eyes. He had never undertaken a lemming — in fact I had never seen one carved — and laughed apologetically when he handed it over, but to me it was perfection: a life-sized, most endearing little creature with a harassed whiskery face and a plump squat bottom, truly something to be held.

Another time I acquired two carvings in a manner so contemporary as to make the purists pale twice over: I could find no walrus or bear that really satisfied among the Co-op carvings, and I told Annakudlip this. Where could I find a walrus that was not skimpy, a bear of note? Annakudlip beamed, "Two, three days, plenty bear and walrus," he said, and pointed out of the door to the radio shack. "I send out after news, tell carvers. How big you want them?" So I showed him with my hands, and three days later Mukpa arrived with a walrus of most solidly pleasing folds, then Mary Allalooh with a bear carved in a very light gray stone, a bear in a hurry, intent on something, his great flowing weight taken lightly on his inturned paws. A noteworthy bear indeed.

The other carving in my collection that I love goes to the other extreme, for not only is it very contemporary but it is huge — over a hundred pounds of soapstone, a hunter struggling within the enclasping paws of a bear. I can hardly keep my hands off the great fluid curve of the massive hindquarters. It was carved by Mary Allalooh too. Almost everything she did had the same great strength and simplicity.

A lot of the carving at Pond was done by women. On a windless sunny day they would sit outside their houses, or sometimes on the grassy headland below the kindergarten, banging and sawing away — it is essential that this part be done outside because of the fine dust — the baby back in the amouti undisturbed, even though it looked as though it might fall out of the hood sometimes when the mother bent over more closely to her work.

The carvings were priced by a committee of Eskimos, and were then either put on the shelves of the Co-op hut or packaged up at the crafts center at the school to go to Ottawa, where they were distributed to various outlets with a hundred percent markup on the prices. The Co-op hut on Thursdays, when the newest carvings were on the shelves, was always in a pleasant state of chaos, with Annakudlip rummaging around for a lost price tag or a bit of paper with the carver's name, or openly skeptical about the quality of some work, rolling his eyes heavenward at the price. (He had a Portuguese grandfather which accounted for his unusually narrow and expressive face.) Pond Inlet sculpture had a very good name in the south, despite the fact that a good deal of the work of the few great carvers never found its way out, either being bought by the white residents or others in the know. Price was not always indicative of excellence, for the committee knew that some names could command more; but where Seana, for example, might carve something magnificently priceless in April, he could well have an off day in March and the committee not notice the difference. In fact some of the little unsigned objects, many of them first attempts by youngsters and priced as low as fifty cents, were the most rewarding in terms of "art," simple and refreshing in contrast to the sometimes crudely overworked pieces at the lowest end of the selling scale of their elders.

The soapstone varied considerably from source to source, so that most people could tell immediately where such and such a piece was from, the texture varying in its hardness, the colors from black to olive or lighter green. Pond soapstone came from an outcrop about sixty miles away, brought by boat and dumped on the beach, the biggest blocks being about eighteen inches square. There were always plenty of bits lying around, and as it is really a soft talc in rock form, even my usually blunt penknife could make an impression.

Pieces used to be signed on the bottom only by the Eskimo's number, such as E. 19–256–7, or the name in syllabics; more recently the name follows the number in ordinary script. The E. (for Eskimo) numberings were the only method the Department of Northern Affairs could use for their files, as there were no surnames. However, 1971 was a census year in Canada, and it was insisted then that all Eskimos who had not yet decided on a family surname must pick one for the census forms. Hence the E. identification will now fade out. Much confusion reigned at Pond over this while I was there, the administration having to cope with the strange and often fanciful new names that appeared on the forms.

It became even more complicated when Colly Scullion found that she had to obtain passports for the Eskimo Guides that she was taking to a world meeting in Greenland: Ottawa was very cooperative and passports were about to be issued quickly with the new names, but it was then found that two of the girls had been "given" to their families and so were not really entitled to the name at all, and this had to be sorted out.

Children were given, and still are, to other families for various reasons: perhaps an ill balance of the sexes, so that a particular family needs a daughter to help the mother or a son to hunt with the father; perhaps an elderly widowed aunt, or a grandmother needs the interest in, and help from, a young person. Mostly this works out very satisfactorily, but sometimes loyalties conflict with progress. A good example was a boy in Pond, now sixteen, who had been given to his grandmother. He should be going out to Frobisher Bay to the high school there to complete his education, yet he cannot leave her, for she is now old and frail and needs him.

Children "given" this way nowadays must be legally adopted. John, in his capacity as a Justice of the Peace, filled in the necessary forms, setting the wheels in motion; then the forms were sent to the judge in Yellowknife, and the whole thing was quite simple. There were never any orphan children — they were always taken in by a family, to become as much a part of it as "given" children, indistinguishable from blood relatives.

Illegitimate children were rare, but whether this was because the efficacy of the birth control pill was being demonstrated even here — in the more sophisticated, accessible settlements of the western Arctic it is dished out as a matter of course even to fourteen-year-olds — or because Pond was just naturally more straitlaced, I don't know. Certainly there was little outward evidence of promiscuity. One of its most remarkable aspects, in fact, was the complete absence on the village scene of any boy-girl relationship: boys played together, girls played together, but teen-age boy was never seen with teen-age girl and I never once saw the springtime horseplay or moony wanderings-

around-together of the south. I do not know where courting
went on, as it must have; probably in homes, although once I
passed a tent pitched on the cliffs before the last houses in the
village and heard the sound of familiar teen-age giggling from
within; and once the hatch door on an old wreck of a boat
opened and shut quickly when I happened to turn round on my
way back from fishing at Quilalukan. Perhaps, too, one does
not see young couples here because they marry so early; what
one thinks might be a teen-age girl with her baby sister in her
amouti hood is probably very often a married woman with her
own child.

❧ Chapter 4 ❧

At the same time as the migrant birds returned to the Arctic, the first flocks of various field specialists flew up there too, cramming their activities as frenziedly into the same short season, dispersing to lonely tents and huts scattered up and down the Northwest Territories, from Frobisher to the Pole: glaciologists, biologists, archaeologists, anthropologists, entomologists, ecologists — every possible -ologist, including enthusiasts who fixed tiny transmitters on Mergansers or tags on polar bears, studied musk ox droppings, thermokarp, caribou parasites or the social life of lemmings. Sometimes a planeload of them landed briefly at Pond, weather-strayed or outward bound to some scientific Ultima Thule — mainly a delightful flock of interesting, diffident individualists, with well worn packsacks and a strange variety of shabbily practical garb. From their patient, painstaking study eventually will come a deeper understanding of the northern ecology — not only what makes it tick but what must be done to stop it running down.

In the last year or two these summer migrants have inevitably been joined by a new but increasing species: the oil men, probing every corner too, but not so altruistically. The oil men usually arrived in quartet form in sleek company planes or

helicopters, and looked as though they had sprung thus, fully
accoutered and clad, from the same well: large yellow boots,
peaked caps, unblemished unbaggy parkas, and clean white
socks. All had lean, clean-shaven jaws, so firmly set that one
suspected they might have been locked before departure by
their company security officer as a precaution against oral oil
spillage.

Usually one only saw them in rapid transit if one happened
to be up at the airstrip. One morning, however, woken by rude
noise, I looked out of my window to find an expressionless quartet hovering in a plastic bubble before it. I probably looked
baleful. They descended from eye level, as though going down
on a very slow elevator, and came to rest on a small flat space
below: the Pan-Texan-Gulf helicopter had arrived. Thence-
forward, for the next few days, it came and went at all hours,
shattering my peace inside, while outside the unfortunate huskies
and poppies clung on grimly before the sand-blasting hurricane
from the slipstream.

But, to be honest, it wasn't the disturbance that riled me so
much — or even their nefarious business — it was pure green-
eyed jealousy: that they had the means to go where *I* wanted
to go but couldn't get to. Every time they took off and up they
whirled straight across the ice to Bylot, and within minutes
they were flying up the white sweep of my glacier immediately
opposite, growing smaller and smaller until they turned up one
of the tributary roads that I had followed so often with my
binoculars, and disappeared into the network of valleys beyond
— into the unseen part of Bylot, hovering down wherever they
wanted, seeing things that I wanted to see. . . .

Just to the left of that glacier at Iglootishak were limestone
cliffs where, it was said, one might find the round concretions
that the people here called juggling stones; there were birds
and wild flowers there that were not to be found here; there

had been tantalizing mention of a huge fossilized tree trunk seen from the air in one of those valleys; and there was the mystique of the ancient ice cap and those sheer white peaks, so often veiled in cloud from here. I don't often suffer from jealousy, but I had looked across to Bylot so long and often that it had become an obsession. And, as though to tease me further, a seal hunt arranged with Muqtar, to be combined with a landing ashore to explore the limestone cliffs, had twice fallen through because the ice conditions had become too treacherous.

Then, just when I had given up all hope for that year at least (I had even sunk so low as to try smiling ingratiatingly as any hitchhiker in the direction of the helicopter, but to no avail), fate sent the gooseman winging into Pond one evening.

I had heard of the elusive gooseman, and often seen the little red Beaver with the outsize tires heading in from the direction of Eclipse Sound, but thought that I would have to wait to meet him until he came to collect the frozen meat, labeled with his name, stowed in our refrigerator. Only defective equipment, a bundle of washing or the need of a shower tore him away from his geese on Bylot. This time it was a camera part, and kindly Heidi, Rick Hamburg's wife, swiftly engineered our meeting over supper.

He was Doug Heyland, an ornithologist from the Quebec Wildlife Service. That night he explained something of his particular project, which was now into its second or third season: an aerial survey of the breeding grounds of the greater snow goose. He was using an entirely new technique of photographing the terrain in a grid system with a twelve-inch focal length, nine-inch format camera fitted to the underbelly of the Beaver, flying up and down the grid at a 1,600-foot altitude. The results were then superimposed and the white dots of geese pinpointed onto a topographical mosaic of film. It was a project in which time was always breathing down his neck, either predictably,

from the amount to be covered in the short season, or frustrat-
ingly, from flying time lost due to bad weather or a breakdown
in equipment. He had a university student, Stanley George, as
his assistant, up here for his third year running as a summer
job; and the pilot was John Seznick, a medical student from
Minnesota. The trio were camped at Ujarasugyulik, where Navy
Board Sound merges into Eclipse Sound, almost on the spot
where the "savssat" of narwhal and beluga described by
Christian Vibe occurred.

There and then he suggested that we come over and see for
ourselves what was going on in Gooseland; there was a spare
tent, just bring sleeping bags and food. It was as simple as that.
He would send a radio message next time John Seznick came
over to refuel; it would give us nice time to get up to the airstrip; just be ready to jump aboard the Beaver, as it would leave
again immediately. He could have saved himself the last instruction: I would have stood on the strip with my track shoes
on day and night indefinitely for a ticket to Gooseland.

But of course in the end the simple turn-around operation did
not occur as scheduled; it never does in the North; there one
soon learns to have a meal in one pocket and a paperback in
the other. We panted up the hill with sleeping bags and packs
at 4:30, as per radio message, and the Beaver arrived a few
minutes later. But it was a busy day at Pond: a Texas Gulf
plane had arrived to refuel as well. Its yellow boots must have
marched off to inspect the aboriginals' carvings, and the pilot
was probably having a cup of tea at the nursing station, for
there was no one around except some little boys and the be-
mused owner of a Piper Aztec who had dropped in for no
apparent reason, taxied off the strip, and was now disconsolately
surveying the wheels of his machine, which were well and truly
bogged down below the heather.

In due course the oil men were rounded up, and the pilot

appeared, and as John helped him to refuel, the Piper owner, trying to be helpful, filled our tanks — unfortunately from the wrong barrel, with dirty car gas. It was obviously not his day. John, looking sulfurous, had to drain the tanks and change the filters. In the meantime, before anyone remembered to commandeer their muscle power, the oil men took off; the little boys now had to be rounded up, and with their enthusiastic help the Piper was eventually heaved and shoved back onto the airstrip. It was now about eight o'clock; Doug would be fit to be tied at the loss of flying hours, said John grimly, as we took off at last.

But to me, with no nagging urgency, the delay in hours meant only that one looked down over the land at a time when all color and shape was enhanced by mellower light and longer shadows.

We flew quite low over Eclipse, where snow, ice and open water had formed into wonderful mosaics, then along the Bylot coast, studded with huge cartwheel impressions, the ice cracks radiating like perfect spokes from the small black rounds of random seal holes. When we rounded the coast and turned up Navy Board Sound, it was possible at last to get an idea of the full majesty of the glaciers sweeping down to the flat of the tundra plains before the coast. There were white dots in pairs and groups criss-crossing the darkness of land all round; and on occasional small lakes the dots were densely massed into almost perfect circles — these were the unmated geese, who would remain together, segregated from the nesting sites on land, and leaving the water only to feed.

The camp could not have been more ideally situated: by the banks of a shallow, gravelly, fast-flowing river, and at the far end of half a mile or so of the tundra extending from the coast to the rise of hills beyond, making a perfect natural airstrip — as long as one had extra-large tires to take up the heathery bumps. It was very shipshape, with a Maple Leaf fluttering from the radio aerial (notwithstanding a pair of pajamas streaming out from one of the stays below); two small blue tents, precisely in line, flanked a Parcoll hut, a new conception in Arctic portable homes, designed to withstand the severest cold. It was shaped like the slice off a Nissen hut, about six by eight feet, with four windows, the whole structure folding ingeniously into the flat boxes which made the floor. This was the radio room, mess tent, galley, office, recreation hall, and sleeping quarters for two all rolled into one. Behind the hut boxes of food and equipment were stacked, everything weighted down with boulders. A canvas-screened privy stood primly at attention about fifty yards away, a spade properly straight at its side. Its zippered door faced over the river to the hills, and a further feature was the small zippered porthole, thoughtfully inset in the door about halfway up. For washing facilities there was the river.

The panorama was like nothing I could ever have imagined. No quarter of the horizon perimeter remotely resembled the others, yet all flowed without any break in harmony into the whole of the flower-bright tundra and the changing patterns of ice. Far behind the camp the pure white peaks of the ice field rose in spectacular isolation from the dark mountains, the low rays of the midnight sun striking almost at a level; far before, rimming Navy Board Sound to the west, was another magnificent range of mountains, which were not only majestic bastions in their own right but had the additional fascination of changing shape completely. When I first saw them they were completely flat on top, like table land, some with jutting-out flatnesses, like the serried decks of an aircraft carrier, and some with squared-off catwalks leading to nowhere. I photographed them there and then — much to Doug's amusement: I had been completely fooled by a temperature inversion. The next time I

looked they were all the right way up again, crags and but-
tresses pointing properly to the sky. They have remained that
way ever since among my photographs, sadly, for I liked them
better the other way.

This was the land that Susan and I and the nesting birds were
to have to ourselves most of the time, for the Beaver was air-
borne almost all the working days, only returning briefly at
lunchtime, sometimes gone until the evening if they refueled at
Pond and stayed there for supper. Then we would use the comfort of the hut ourselves to eat and read and work in; or,
instructed in the use of the shortwave set, have a prearranged
chat with Doug in the Beaver. When the wind rose and blew
without ceasing for the third day, we were thankful for our
haven, snug and warm within, while without our tent flapped
like a mad thing and the wind howled past the aerial mast
making strange singing music in the stays. Every time I fell
asleep within those wildly straining, flapping nylon walls I embarked on the same dream sailing boat and we set off once
again into the teeth of a gale, endlessly coming about, very
badly, with a shuddering snap of sails. It wasn't even as though
I could look forward to getting somewhere on the next installment, for we never seemed to make any progress. Sometimes,
however, we jibed, which was a good thing, for then I would
wake up in time to struggle out and secure whichever guy rope
had parted from its boulder.

Even the sewn-in floor between the cots was in constant
motion. It must have been pitched over the main thoroughfare
of some very active lemming community, rippling busily as the
inhabitants went about their business. Sometimes I would put
my finger gently on a small traveling hump and watch it accel-
erate madly down its highway.

Usually when I woke up I stayed awake — reluctant both to
continue the sea saga and to waste any time in Shangri-La.

Then I would stretch out on the cot with my head by the door, unzip an inch or so of tent and watch the life on the sunlit tundra through field glasses, a deluxe form of bird-watching. At this level, too, if I turned the glasses on the ground just a few yards away I had a delightfully different ant's-eye perspective of that most unfortunately named, but most attractive flower, the lousewort. It was the woolly lousewort in particular that was such a memorable feature of the tundra. Sturdy and straight, rearing in high isolation above the white nodding bells of heather, it made a single exotic splash of color against the dark greens and browns. The pink, mauve or blue flowerets leaned out in neat tiers to form an enviably warm white fluff — a most practical Arctic arrangement. The long yellow root had a pleasant taste, a cross between carrot and turnip. (One can, if one has a mind to, eat any wild flower, root, berry or mushroom in the Arctic zone — nothing is poisonous. I was always munching there.)

Most of the flowers seemed to be adapted in one way or another to the extreme cold or wind, some so ingeniously arranged that they could go into a kind of suspended state if overcome too early in their reproductive period, to resume activities at a more suitable occasion, or even the following year; and most of them are insulated by hairs or down, and rely on the wind for pollination, as there would not be enough arctic bees or butterflies to do the job.

Between beach and tent, marked with little red pennants, only about fifty yards away, were the almost completely camouflaged nests of two pairs of ruddy turnstones, beautiful little harlequins in their spring plumage; and nearby a pair of black-bellied plovers, as lovely, but in a more sophisticated simplicity of dress. I spent many hours watching and filming them; the covert, hurried creeping away at my approach to lure me away from the nest, the exhausted sinking to earth with its pathetic lowering and raising of a fluttering wing. This was plover behavior. The turnstones were far more naïve with their indignantly melodious "tink, tink, tinks" of protest, running nearer the nest as I neared it myself. Their alarm calls always attracted the neighboring plovers who immediately flew over to add their voices to the defense.

Now that we were well into July, there was a perceptible difference in the arc of the sun. Perhaps the birds were aware of this too, for even if there was no division of twilight or darkness to make them tuck their heads under their wings and snatch a few hours off, it seemed to me that there was a quieting down and a respite from activity among the neighboring plovers and turnstones when the sun dipped to its lowest point.

On the slope above them a pair of longtailed jaegers had their nest. Fiercely protective, aggressively territorial over the surrounding hundred yards, they dive-bombed or came at me from front and rear like aerial torpedoes, so close that I could actually feel them touch my hair. Sometimes they hovered on fast-beating angular wings within a foot of my face, but never did I feel that they would actually strike it. When I left the nest one of them would always see me off to the limits of their territory. If I remained quite still, kneeling on the ground, they would take no notice of me. I used to enjoy watching them make one of their almost hourly sorties around the neighboring nests, uttering their high-pitched hunting cry, such noisy braggarts that the parents of any potential meal were well warned in advance, and had time to rush back to their territory, warn their mates, then fly out to their borders to repel the raider — who, though twice the size, always retreated before the barrage of insults.

They were most confusing birds — farther down the river nested a pair of parasitic jaegers, almost uniformly dark, yet across the river was a pair in what the *Field Guide* called the "light phase," with black caps and strikingly white undercarriage, and, apart from their short pointed tail feathers, very like the pomarine from a distance.

Arctic terns nested on the gravel spits of the river too. Fairytale birds they seemed, particularly when I watched them over the gleaming pinnacles and turrets of the ice castles lining the shore, with their blood-red beaks and long forked tails. Hovering brilliant white against a blue sky, they could suddenly wheel and turn so fast that I could not keep them covered in the camera lens. Or they would stoop for a fish with a speed beyond even my naked eye's capability of following.

Down here, too, where the estuary flowed out and under the ice, I could often watch a red-throated loon. For the first time I saw them in full plumage, or close enough in flight to appreciate how long and snakelike were the head and neck. Furthermore, although I never found the nest, the male — or I took it to be the male — once or twice obligingly sat near enough on a small pond for me to photograph him so that I could check out his distinguishing points at my leisure in Peterson's invaluable *Field Guide.*

Beyond the estuary there were miles of beautiful beaches, whose fine soft white sand was scattered with the bleached-smooth bones of seal and whale. What driftwood there was could be picked up and put in one's pocket, tiny gnarled branches of dwarf willow, sand-polished to satin smoothness. Against the immensity of their setting they were as incongruous as was the realization that there would be no waves lapping here for weeks yet. This was an *Arctic* beach, but sometimes the sand was so warm that I went barefoot, and all along the curving unimprinted coast line a purple carpet of saxifrage bordered the banks.

One day when I was stretched out on the sand, enjoying the

Arctic equivalent of a sunbath — that part of the face unob-
scured by sunglasses, and the forearms — John Seznick suddenly appeared over the bank and along the beach on a Trail-
breaker, a kind of super-motorcycle with chain-drive wheels and
enormous deeply treaded tires. I rode back to the camp, bump-
ing over the heather on the pillion seat. There were two of these
machines parked by the hut, capable of going anywhere in this
terrain — straight up mountains or through quagmires. They
were used here for visiting outlying nests — or, as today, to
fetch me back because Doug was ravening for his supper.

(Doug was always ravenous on terra firma, and we had huge,
hearty meals there: thin as a rake, he could knock back two
steaks, a bowl of potatoes and a mountain of vegetables and
still look hopefully around for more. Always trying to beat the
clock, he was understandably tense and hyperactive on the job,
burning up energy like an express train; refueled, he was the
most relaxed, amusing and witty character, and endlessly patient in explaining to lay ears the complexities of his work.)

All this life and activity took place on the tundra plateau. Up
beyond the gentle rise of hills was another world altogether.
There, from the crest one looked down on a valley widely
forked by a curving river, the far side sloping up again in long
fields, a world verdant and pastoral. Scattered all over the hillsides and river meadows were the pairs of nesting geese, snow-
white save for the orange-red stains of iron oxide on their necks
from their winter feeding grounds. If I walked up the river
where it wound close to the little cliffs, long necks rose like
periscopes against the skyline and curious heads peered down,
and others, out for a feed and a change of scene, rose leisurely
at my approach and flew back to the nest, sometimes turning
and passing so close that one could almost stretch out and touch
them. It was like some legendary hidden valley, sunlit and

tranquil. Yet only a few miles farther into the interior, beneath the ice cap, lay hills and valleys that had not known the sun for a thousand years.

On the very top of a hill, commanding a view of both forks of the valley and the river, was a snowy owl's nest. No nest could have been more thoughtfully sited, for not only was there a steep, clifflike approach around three sides of it, but handily situated within six feet was a small mound plentifully pierced by lemming tunnels — a kind of living larder. A pair of geese nested within fifteen feet, and seemed to be on most neighborly terms with the owls. I had heard that the geese are only too delighted to share their terrain with owls as they made such excellent guards against weasels and other predators, and certainly there was never any such alarm shown here when the snowies swooped back and forth from their hunting sorties as there was if the jaegers appeared. But I certainly saw the remains of a gosling snack in the nest one day, along with the more mundane lemming course. (However, one should always be charitable about this sort of find: perhaps it was a particularly puny gosling that had expired naturally — blown out of the nest? — and the owls were just tidying things up.

The first day I went there, Mrs. Owl rose from the nest immediately and took off on her great silent wings across the valley. There were seven eggs, and one quite large owlet, probably hatched the day before, sprawled across them in quite amazingly unattractive nakedness. It seemed to be all beak and enormous feet. I photographed it as quickly as possible, for the male owl was swooping around rather too closely for my comfort, crossly clicking his beak. I retreated down the steep hillside until I was out of sight of the nest, and watched him reconnoiter while I ate my lunch. When I stood at last, and peeped round a corner at the nest above, it was to see Mrs. Owl craning far out of it, glaring down at me with saucer-eyed indignation.

She took off at once, but this time returned quite quickly. I stayed where I was to reassure her, and for the next hour we played a kind of peek-a-boo, she remaining on the nest and gradually less uneasy.

During the next two days the pattern was much the same, as long as I kept to the agreed distance; but on the last day, when she was four owlets down and four to go, her reaction to my arrival was really no more than a token gesture — a quick flap out and around and back. She and I and Mrs. Snow Goose next door had become so companionable by this time, all girls together, that I found myself almost fluffing out the hem of my parka as I sank down on my lunch nest below. Sometimes my lunch was not too different from that of the geese, for after the invariable Pilot biscuit-and-cheese-and-raisins I usually finished off with some of the little brown berrylike roots of the Alpine bistort (*polyginum viviparum*) dug up from the river meadows, and from the little patches of turf dug up and cast aside, just like mine, it seemed that the geese shared my taste for the cachou nutlike flavor.

Many of the goose nesting sites were marked with the little red flags planted there by Doug and Stan to ascertain if the same site would be used the following year. One particular area of grassland, flat, then undulating, looked not unlike a golf course some days, each hole marked by the unvarying shapes of one goose standing and one goose sitting. The nests were loosely constructed from bits of heather and other vegetation, and lined with down. The first evening I visited the sites they contained anywhere from four to seven eggs. (I learned later that the earlier geese lay the larger clutch; the young geese always lay late and consequently have the ultimate responsibility of fewer goslings to rear; no eggs are laid after June 6 or 7). The eggs were all completely covered by down if the parents were away, or had had time to nudge the feathers over with their beaks before departing at our approach. One nest only showed signs of the frenetic activity that would take place over the next few days, containing one gosling so newly hatched that it was still damp, one egg with a beak within widening the crack, and a third egg that cracked as we watched to the urgent little tappings from inside. Two lazier eggs remained as yet intact. I filmed these minor miracles, then carefully covered them up again with down.

Next day the parents did not fly away but walked, very slowly and agitatedly, for there were three little fluffy, yellow balls trying to keep up with them, stumbling and falling between their runs. In the nest was the latest member of the family, barely dry, and the last egg had a crack with a determined beak getting to work. By morning there were five little yellow balls following the parents, who were already beginning to look harassed. It did not seem fair to add to their worries with my presence, so I left quickly; although I would have liked to follow them all day, and to watch the goslings feeding, perhaps even swimming.

It was impossible to identify this particular family thereafter, for the nesting site is vacated for good when the last gosling is dry and on its feet, and the hillsides and meadows were already becoming like some park on a Bank Holiday, with all the other parents and their straggling lines of children. I had to watch very carefully where I put my boots. When the wind blew, which it did without ceasing for the last two days, twenty-four hours a day, the goose families on the crest of the hill had a nerve-wracking time: the poor little goslings who had just climbed over the sides of the nest into the outside world were often bowled along the bare gravelly parts, sometimes being halted in time only by a providential tuft of grass before being wafted into space over the edge of the cliff, sometimes being

fielded smartly by one or other of the parents. Not being of a
precocial species, Mrs. Owl's children remained in the nest, dependent on their parents for a long time, and so were in no
danger; but she had a most trying time, as her feather carpets
and covers kept flying off every time she left home, and she was
constantly having to replenish them.

But at least the wind seemed to restrict the predatory jaegers
to lemmings only, for during that time I saw none of the usual
pattern of disturbance which had been such a feature of the
still days: the peaceful pastoral scene with the same dual blobs
of white scattered over the green land, and only the sounds of
plovers and the river, everything domesticated and peaceful —
then suddenly, the first shrill warning notes of the jaeger, and
the whole pattern would change instantly: lines criss-crossing,
angry necks outstretched in pairs, and a general uproar all
round until the hunters left, and peace would reign again. I
noticed that the geese disregarded my presence completely
when the jaegers were around. Only a comparatively small
number of nests had broken empty eggs lying nearby, which
was a tribute to their vigilance.

Down by the river toward the shore was the nest of a pair of
geese who were either a teen-age romance or dropouts from
society, for they were far removed from the protection of their
fellows. Things were in a shocking state around the site — five
plundered eggs, and only two left within the nest. The parents
always seemed to be slouching around the tundra, with just an
occasional perfunctory sit-in and stand-on-guard routine —
both looking slightly surprised as they took it up, as though
they had no idea what prompted them in the first place. The
long-tailed jaegers nearby had it made — for needless to say
this improvident pair had them as their nearest neighbors. I had
become so engrossed in all the bird family life around that I

longed to pick this pair up when I saw them on their wanderings, shake them until their beaks rattled, plonk them back
down on nest duty, and tell them to get with it.

I used to feel rather ashamed of my lack of detached, factual
observation, particularly in such rarefied company, in a hut
which was stuffed with scientific data. But Doug was kind
enough to say that he could fall prey to anthropomorphism too,
and mentioned a goose called Mabel who had been a very
close neighbor last year, and after that I relaxed, and enjoyed
the greater snow goose my own way.

It was a time divorced of reality and any pressure of thought.
Perhaps that is why I was so deeply disturbed when the only
element of reality intruded, because the contrast was of my own
civilized interpretation, imported with me. It happened the first
evening. I had gone out with Stan on a tour of the nesting sites,
and we were walking back over the brow of the hill when he
suddenly stopped and pointed, and for a moment my heart
missed a beat for I could see a large white head just over the
hummock about a hundred yards away. My mind was just registering — polar bear: do I run, stand, walk away, film . . .
when the head turned and I saw two round black eyebrow
markings: it was a huge husky dog. John appeared and waved
at us to skirt it, shouting that they didn't want it to follow us
back to camp. The dog crouched against the hillside, watching
us steadily, licking its flank, and I saw now that it had a tattered canvas harness on. It had come down from the hills and
swum across the river, making for the hut, but had been driven
off from there to this hummock.

From time to time for the next two hours, I turned my field
glasses on the hillside: the dog never moved from its place,
only licking the wounded leg, then raising its head to stare
steadily at the campsite. Shortly after we had gone into our
tent for the night and the men were inside, it rose, very stiffly,

and limped down the hill and across the tundra toward the camp. When it saw me at the tent flap the dog hesitated, then halted, about a hundred yards away now. He was still in his thickest winter coat; but through the glasses I saw that the coat was shabby and worn down to the skin in places, and that he was old.

Then, to my horror, he wagged his tail. I wish he hadn't. I wish he had looked at me with all the cold indifference that Eskimo dogs show toward a stranger. But this one was so desperate to placate any human being that he wagged his tail.

One of the men erupted from the hut, fired a shot into the air, and yelled, "Scram, you lousy dirty old bag of bones," then, half apologetically, to us, "If we once give it something we'll have it for good, and there won't be a thing safe when we're up in the air — it'll pillage the lot." He was quite right, and I knew what was going to happen, and knew it was the only thing to do and the most merciful, because there was no longer any place for this dog in the order of things: this was the Arctic, not suburbia; nor was it an execution without trial, but a practical procedure.

So I reasoned. Yet this husky, who had wagged his tail so uneasily before us just now, was a dog who had lived and worked in the cruelest possible elements for his entire life, straining his heart out in harness, goaded on by the whip lash, or staked out to a short chain in the nonworking months, to fight and pant with thirst with his team, his only reward the hunk of seal or fish flung down once or twice a week, his only anticipation that of running in the traces again. In spite of all this, in his extremity he had sought out man again — and heaven knows how far or for how long the search had been on this uninhabited island — and shown by the only means in his power that he was ready to do the whole thing over again.

But we had no use for him. At another threat, he dragged

himself back a few yards, then, when once again there was no movement outside the hut, he regained the ground. John came out with a rifle, and lay down to take aim. The dog wagged his tail again, there was a crack, and he fell. There was no movement, only the stiff, injured hind leg lowering slowly down to the heather. He had known nothing; he was all right now.

But I was not all right, not at peace. I had known something. And what I knew I did not like or understand: the whole human race, of which I was a part.

The wind, the only other disturbing element of a very different kind in this Arctic paradise, blew as I have never before known wind to blow: there seemed to be no shelter anywhere outside from it. It was as though one were the center of a compass with the wind blowing simultaneously from every point: no matter in what direction I went it sought me out and blew straight at me. The only time I did not have to fight it with every breath was when I lay flat on the ground. This seemed to fox it, and it would veer off a point or two in search (in sole occupancy of so much world one tended to come to such primary conclusions). At first I thought it exhilarating, a refreshing breeze that would keep the mosquitoes down, but after two days I had grown to hate it, and to long for even ten minutes' respite when everything outside the tent did not have to be anchored down with boulders, nor papers nor hats retrieved from the outermost ends of the tundra. It was a piercingly cold wind too, and of such velocity at times that I could not hold the camera still enough to photograph.

It was still pursuing us when we climbed into the Beaver to return, slamming the door in frustration and giving us a bumpy ride for the first few minutes. When we got out at Pond, the sky was blue and cloudless, the open water was mirror still, the pack ice unmoving. There had been no wind for days, we were told.

When we next saw Doug he told us that it had stopped abruptly at 4 A.M. two or three days after we left. They all woke up and couldn't go back to sleep again in the silence.

I could understand; we had found the silence of Pond so deafening, the stillness so still that it felt as though something momentous must be about to burst on us any moment, and when we spoke we shouted. But at least I went no more asailing in that frightful dream boat.

❧ *Chapter 5* ❧

We had bacon and eggs for supper — murres' eggs from the cliffs at Agpah. They are beautiful; about the size of duck eggs, and varying tremendously in color from pale blue with black specks to almost-turquoise, mapped with large black continents. They were well worth every cent of the few cents we paid Muqtar, when one thinks of the effort of getting them: climbing a rope against a vertical cliff to rob the nests, then transporting the eggs back, wrapped in grass, on a thudding komatik. No particular taste, just a feeling that they were very rich — too rich for me; I could only manage half, but Susan managed to down two. The yolks are a brilliant orange.

At least that was quite interesting — murres' eggs are exotic fare; and so perhaps one can defend:

Seal stew tonight. I don't care if I never eat seal stew again. It always tastes of seal, and the texture is gruesome . . . [or even] Heavenly dinner at Scullions — musk ox, potatoes, peas . . . etc., etc.

But all the other carefully detailed accounts, down to the last Pilot biscuit, of every snack — or obvious droolings over the presence of an onion, a loaf of bread, the remains of some shepherd's pie from the construction crew's cook; the transports of joy over an orange, half a cabbage . . . I had not realized until I reread my journals what an obsession about food is manifest there. Yet I distinctly remember becoming a little bored occasionally with the endless gastronomic details in all the books of Arctic exploration that I read at the time ("dinner time — rejoiced in pickled cabbage and dried peaches. . . ." "The pot was kept boiling and the igloos rang with primitive joy. . . ." "It was a glorious meal (dog, as far as I remember); we ate forgetful of the past, and almost heedless of the future. . . ."), and can only conclude that either something of this literary style washed off on me, or that good healthy Arctic air just naturally develops an appetite like a horse. . . .

We had received all kinds of advice about food before leaving, ranging from having supplies freighted up beforehand to buying especially dehydrated complete meals, or taking sackloads of vitamin pills; so in the end one did nothing except take along a bag of onions and apples the first year, bitterly regretting them almost immediately when it came to paying excess baggage at a dollar a pound, and in the end we ate extremely well, if a little unusually.

I never became addicted to seal meat — although the liver was delicious — and entirely agree with Kane's description of it: "When raw the meat has a flabby look, more like coagulated blood than muscular fibre; cooking gives it a dark soot colour; it has . . . a flavour of lamp-oil." The blubber was unexpectedly good, of a delightful, melting-in-the-mouth, almost nonexistent texture, and with no more taste than mineral oil — a sensation more than a taste. Muktuk, the narwhal skin, was good from the first bite — a flavor of hazel nuts — and the taste for it grew and grew. And Arctic char is fit for the gods, whether raw or cooked — although I couldn't bring myself to try that tastiest of all parts, apparently, the eyes, which the Eskimos suck out with gusto. Musk ox to me was not unlike horse, although possibly a little richer, and caribou rather

duller than venison. (There were no musk ox on Baffin — the
herd is on Ellesmere Island.) We would usually get fresh bread
from one of the Eskimo women who baked it twice a week, and
for the rest of the time there was bannock, the flour-and-baking-
soda substitute made in a frying pan.

The most exciting source of food came from the leftovers or
handouts from the construction crew's cooks, based next door.
Someone should write a book about northern cooks: they are a
race unto themselves. And so are the work crews for that matter.
It takes a particular type to sign on for these northern tours.
They go wherever they are sent by the Department of Northern
Affairs on building work, and may be away for anything up to
six months. The pay is especially good, with plenty of overtime
— and most of them want overtime as there is nothing for them
to do with their free time in these small settlements: no pubs,
TV, or movies — except for the weekly film showings; dalliance
with village maidens very definitely frowned upon, and the possibility that they could have temperamental companions, or,
worse still, a temperamental cook. (There was a cook at Clyde
River who did not like to be spoken to until after breakfast, and
threw whatever he had to hand at anyone committing this
social error — eggs, the toaster, sausages or milk — and it was
just too bad if you happened to be a stranger in the midst and
didn't know the form: you got the scrambled eggs in your face
just the same. But he was a good cook, and as such to be
humored.)

We were very lucky both years, with first Louis Domina, then
Ulrich, the latter having a mainly French Canadian crew. Pond
was lucky too, for in such a small community an influx of five
or six men has quite a bearing on many aspects of village life,
particularly if there are malcontents or would-be Don Juans
among them.

I went in a few minutes ago to borrow their kettle, as our oil stove
had expired, and they were all sitting tidily around the table, with a
frilly plastic table cloth, having coffee and pie, like children at school,
Louis Domina at the head of the table in spotless white, and came
out with the kettle, two oranges and some cold chicken. The kitchen
is always immaculate; and glorious, tasty smells drift out: pork or
chicken, all kinds of vegetables and normally unobtainables, for no
expense is spared in feeding the crews really well.

Sometimes Bernadette cooked for other transients, such as the
freezer man on his round of community deep freezes, or the
Bell Telephone man, here to juggle with the innards of Pond's
radiotelephone or the village's own interhouse system. Once she
left her cookery book with me, and I spent an entranced afternoon with it. It made a wonderful change from my usual reading material of books on Arctic expeditions; so much intrepidity,
stoicism, exhaustion, starvation, endurance; so many fatalities
or hairbreadth escapes; wrecked canoes, sinking ships, drifting
ice floes — I used to feel quite pooped by the end of a chapter,
and very hungry. So I fell upon Bernadette's *Northern Cookery
Book* and devoured it from cover to cover — and never have I
come across a cookery book that went straight to my heart as
this one did.

It had been compiled as a Centennial project, with individual
northern cooks contributing their specialties. The range was all-
embracing: if you had the desire to set the Arctic afire with
your culinary fame there was an exotic choice of recipes for
the kindling: Whale Bobotee sounded sensational, Reindeer
Bourguignon could well make a trendy change from Christmas
turkey; then there was the delicate appeal of Ptarmigan Pie, or
mouth-watering Oven-Roasted Lynx . . . the list of gourmet
delights was endless.

But it was the great basic simplicity of method and ingredients in the majority of recipes that reached right out of the

pages to me. Take that Oven-Roasted Lynx, for example: no fooling around with basting or parsley or roux-making; just two starkly practical lines: "Wash and clean the hind legs of lynx and roast in a roaster with lard and a little water."

And for those who resent dancing attendance on a saucepan or oven when they could be elsewhere doing a thousand better things, or for those who have a tendency to forget and let things boil dry, like me, Boiled Smoked Beaver came as a relaxed and leisurely miracle: "Smoke the beaver for a day or two, then cut up the meat and boil it until it is done." There was the same comforting vagueness of time, combined with real thriftiness, in Fried Meat and Leftover Porridge: "Fry the meat and when done add left-over porridge. Cook a little longer."

But Boiled Reindeer Head had the most appeal for me, for all one's ill nature at the prospect of preparing a meal could be vented in the therapy of its preparation. All one needs, beside the reindeer head, is an ax and some cold water. "Skin the head. Then chop it in quarters, splitting it between the eyes with an axe. Cover with cold water and boil until soft."

Then there was Seal-in-a-Bun, Dorothy Mackintosh's Moose, Steamed Muskrat Legs (this one had an interesting slant on the use of seasonings, for the legs must be dipped in a bowl of flour with salt and pepper, and any "strong seasoning" available. Further along the recipe candidly reveals the reason: "the strong seasoning takes away the actual taste of the muskrat"). There was one short and succinct recipe that I thought put Mrs. Beeton and her grandiose ingredients (take twenty-four eggs, etc.) thoroughly in her place: "Fried Whale Meat: cut up freshly caught whale. Fry in grease with onions."

But I could go on indefinitely, and of course I have picked out the more exotic examples, those that could bring a tired, oversophisticated palate back to life. There were pages and pages of the more prosaic fare normally encountered in a cookery book, although most of these were slanted toward the northern cook's limitations of a once-a-year shopping list, with dried eggs, canned or dehydrated vegetables, and many other ingenious substitutes. Even the household hints at the end had an adventurous northern tang to them: how to render bear fat, loosen doors or windows frozen shut, or locate North if you happen to be lost.

Seal liver and muktuk are very rich in vitamin C. Had my Arctic explorers only left their gastronomic mores behind in their own countries in those early days, history could have been rewritten without the decimation of scurvy. I find it interesting too that despite so much blubber and oil in the diet no Eskimo grows fat; nor do they suffer from the coronary disease that is currently believed to be due to too much cholesterol in the white man's diet.

One thing I found still consistent with early accounts of Eskimo eating habits: the feast or famine principle. No rationing or hoarding of the last seal flipper or piece of pemmican for them: fill up when you can, and let's see what tomorrow brings. This had its dangers, and there are many accounts of the severe effects or even deaths resulting from the sudden gross overdistension of the stomach when, say, a walrus or seal had been killed after days of little or nothing to eat. A friend living in an Eskimo family told me that it was quite common for there to be very little in the house for days, when suddenly someone might appear with seventeen fish: thereupon everyone would gorge until the last fin had disappeared, with no thrifty thoughts of keeping some for tomorrow's supper.

This can be rather trying for the Kabloonah stomach, accustomed to receiving fairly regular supplies of food-fuel. One day we tried to get across to Iglootishak on Bylot, with Joatanee and Isseyuto, two young hunters, reckoning on about eight hours for the round trip, including time to explore the cliffs and the old site. We took along some sandwiches for lunch there, and as a providential afterthought, I filled my pockets with some broken bits of nutritious biscuits which I had found in the kindergarten — the kind of biscuit intended for underprivileged countries, tasting of sawdust but stuffed with every possible vitamin and nutrient. In actual fact we were out on the ice in the bitterest wind for nearly fourteen hours, as the treads on the skidoo were twice severed by the breaking ice, and the engine had internal problems. We turned back halfway, the various repairs fortunately holding out — but we could well have spent the next twenty-four or forty-eight hours on a nasty bleak icepan. Divided among four, the biscuits and sandwiches didn't go far, but at least it was something. But I am quite certain that, by themselves, Joatanee and Isseyuto would not have given a second thought to the fourteen-hour stretch without food. There was a four-pound can of jam in the tea box: they would probably have finished that off, then waited quite happily for the Lord to provide some other sustenance in a day or two.

I suppose the Eskimo people have developed some form of metabolic compensation especially geared to the Arctic conditions. Their movements, particularly those of the men, are far more active than those of white people in general. I don't think I ever saw anyone standing or sitting still simply looking into space. In fact one page of my journal is headed:

Thought for Tonight! That there is a great untapped source of future Olympic material in Eskimo boys: that their broad jump could be record breaking, for little boys by the shore play at jumping ice floes, and even the smallest toddler almost takes off in his own leap. Eskimos may be small, but I swear that they can jump about four times their own length. Then the 100 yards dash: what could be better training for this than leaping off a komatik, flanking the running dogs — and all the time cracking a whip — or overhauling a runaway team going hell-bent for a seal. And sailing, for not only is there a real sense of helmsmanship needed in steering a fast traveling komatik on land, but water is their other environment; from the days of the frail skin kayak to today's canoes with outboards. Anyone who can navigate a 16' canoe or dinghy in Arctic waters with a 14' komatik, a skidoo, eight dogs, one oil drum and an elderly father aboard (as I've just watched from the window) should go places, for their environment is a constant challenge to remain fit. And it's small wonder that they are so fit and active, always running and jumping around, playing "I'll shove you, you shove me" type of athletic horseplay games on the ice: if they didn't they'd freeze to death.

They were not fat, but neither did they appear thin, somehow giving the impression of having a firmer, thicker layer of subcutaneous tissue than white skin. Perhaps this made a better insulation. I don't know, having no scientific proof, but certainly it seemed that even the youngest, fittest white man felt the cold more. As soon as the snow was off the hills, I would see a group of naked boys, their bodies in startling contrast to their "summer" white faces, jumping in and out, dog-paddling around, splashing and having enormous fun in the icy waters of the river. Time and time again I had the impression that the cold was not an enemy; it was simply something not even to be thought about.

Diet has changed of course, with so many of the usual supermarket cans available at the Hudson Bay store (I could never get used to the sight of a hunter trotting briskly home with a carton on his shoulder, a packet of Gleem White or Dream Whip peeping out, and a box of Zesty Pep Corn Flakes resting on a box of ammunition), and soon, no doubt, white flour, sugar and candies will take their toll of the beautiful white teeth. But, in contrast to other northern communities, it seemed that here these innovations supplemented rather than supplanted the old staples of seal, fish, whale and caribou, and that the latter were infinitely preferred.

Pond and some other eastern Arctic communities are possibly unique in this world in that the waters and the land are not yet polluted or overpopulated, so that if need be the people could live entirely off them — provided that the present level of animal and marine life were maintained, lowered appallingly though it is within most hunters' memory. There is virtually no unemployment or any welfare-only type of subsistence: ten percent of the men are government-employed; the rest are listed as trappers and hunters, so that, health and education services apart, I think it could still be an entirely self-supporting community — in an anachronistic, limited sense. By this I mean (I think) that if there were any hippie Eskimos bent on forming a back-to-the-earth, eat-the-basics-that-you-grow-yourself, and sell-your-own-produce commune, they could still make a go of it there. Apart from the existence of resources of food, the natural means to procure it are available, not just the primitive tangible things such as ivory for harpoon heads or sinews for thongs, but the essential example of elders who still could turn their hand to the old skills if necessary, plus the extraordinary natural ingenuity inherent in the Eskimo himself — still. There would be plenty of bartering material to boost the economy, too, in today's market, with carvings, embroidery, the manufacture of sensible northern clothing and footwear, and even a slice of the indigenous tourist industry of guiding, fishing, etc., for the well-heeled sportsman.

There are plans afoot in Pond at present for the Co-op to run a fishing camp for the latter. I do not know how it will work out. I frankly think that the majority of Eskimos are not sufficiently interested in, or (thank heaven) awed by such white people as to attempt to understand or cater to their comfort, needs and whims. This inability to wash their hands with invisible soap may be a deterrent to those who are accustomed to getting deference for their dollar.

The present game laws are on the whole properly slanted toward Eskimo needs as well as conservation. But they will need constant revision, for the balance could be irretrievably upset should there ever be an influx of nonresident sportsmen, now that transport is becoming increasingly easier. Resident white hunters who use their licensing advantages do not amount to more than a handful. Even so, my own feeling is that no potential risk should be taken in these days of vanishing wildlife, and that no licenses should be issued save those to indigenous people. "Sportsman," connoting one who kills food mammals for pleasure, should become as derogatory a term among thinking people as it is now when connoting a big game hunter on a safari. Most of today's younger generation, who are to inherit what is left of the world, already think this way; their comments on trophy-hunters are among some of the most scathing and blistering I have ever heard.

As the laws stand at present, for $25 a nonresident may take three ringed seals,* a white resident for $10 may take ten (only Eskimos may shoot the ookjuk, or bearded seal); for only $10 a nonresident may shoot five of the diminishing number of caribou.

Polar bears may only be shot by Eskimos, although there is an interesting elasticity which makes it possible for the white trophy-hunter to achieve his ambition. The number of bears which may be shot by the men of one settlement is decided upon by the average taken over past years — thus Pond has an

---

* It is important to distinguish clearly among seals because recently international public opinion has brought pressure to bear upon the annual slaughter of harp seals for their fur alone off the Canadian Atlantic coast, resulting in the moral boycott of any sealskin abroad. This boycott has, of course, affected a not unimportant part of the Eskimo economy (the public being unaware of the difference in sealskin) where the skin of ringed seals — the by-product of an Eskimo dietary staple — was used in clothing or mukluks for sale in the south.

allocation of thirteen tags. The skins can fetch between six and eight hundred dollars. However, the Eskimos may decide, among themselves, to sell one of these allocating tags to a white man. This white man must hire the services of the Eskimos as guides, as all hunting must be done by dog sled and team only; the ensuing hunt will then cost him $250 for the license, plus $2,000 to the Eskimo hunting party (this sum is usually split up among the settlement) — and this without even taking into account the considerable cost of his transport up to the Arctic. All in all, by the time he has the bearskin treated and tanned, he would be well advised to undertake the further expenditure of a glass case before the moths get at it. Until that happy day when it becomes as offensive to own a polar bear rug as a tiger skin or a leopard coat, this fleecing of the white sportsman himself is as good an extemporization as any. To those who suggest that the economy of the Eskimos will then be affected, I counter-suggest that we pay them *not* to exercise their hunting privilege; whatever the price, it will be cheap in the end if we can save another species from extinction. Why not let the oil companies foot the bill, in infinitesimal compensation to the land and its true inhabitants for all the wealth which they will take from it? No more than the polar bear does the Eskimo legally own any of his territorial birthright.

It is impossible to mention Arctic oil without thinking of the U.S.S. *Manhattan*, the biggest tanker ever built, whose controversial voyage, attempting to prove that a sea route from the Alaskan oil fields was feasible, had ended only a few miles from Pond (as my bruised and battered body testified on the return from the floe edge) very shortly before we arrived there. I had been reading the daily reports of its progress in the wake of our icebreaker, the *Louis St. Laurent*, with as much dismay as most Canadians, cheering when she got stuck and groaning when she made any progress. It was controversial, not only because of the international aspect of territorial waters (the *Manhattan* flew no courtesy Canadian flag), but because of the disastrous ecological effects of a possible wreck thereafter among the tankers which would follow a successful passage. Controversial, too, because a failure might have promoted the alternative of a pipeline across the tundra, which could have its own disastrous effects, damaging the delicate, irretrievable balance of the thermokarp.

Many of the papers had run a wonderfully dramatic picture of the small figure of an Eskimo on the ice confronting the enormous rearing bows of the *Manhattan*, an igloo just visible. Now I had seen the original of that photograph; Leigh Brintnell had taken it, and the Eskimo was none other than Danielee, who, with my other hunting companions, had obligingly built the igloo for the entertainment of the *Manhattan*'s crew.

Many newspaper reports also gave the idea that the *Manhattan*'s arrival (officially the predetermined goal of her voyage achieved; in actual fact she came to a grinding halt) was positively providential from the viewpoint of the undernourished inhabitants of Pond Inlet, who received the quantities of food given with much choking gratitude. The truth was that everyone had a wonderful time, with a real sightseeing carnival atmosphere. The twenty-five-mile distance made a nice day's outing by skidoo or dog team; the ship's helicopter flew villagers back and forth as well; and everyone returned loaded with anti-starvation goodies like grapefruit and fresh vegetables (which would have gone bad soon anyway and had to be dumped over) and Coca-Cola. The economy of Pond jumped too as a brisk trade was done in carvings. Altogether it was a most welcome arrival for the starving inhabitants of Pond — though even *they* couldn't finish off the mountain of accumulated grapefruit; we were given a nice present of some of it.

❧ Chapter 6 ❧

From such present-day frivolities as grapefruit and helicopters and such ominous auguries as tankers and pipelines, I sometimes turned to the past, simply by walking two miles westward from the village to the mouth of the Salmon River. On its banks was the ancient site of Quilalukan, which means narwhal. There was a good description of it in Rasmussen's Report of the fifth Thule expedition lent me by Father Mary, the Oblate missionary.

And presumably this place is an old important spot for these animals (narwhales) which in the early summer pass through Pond's Inlet in thousands. . . . From olden days this place has been an important winter settlement; a large number of houses bear witness of this; this importance it has retained until comparatively recently: an Eskimo told me that right up to the time when the whalers built permanent stations at Pond's Inlet (1903), Quilalukan was the most important winter residence of the Eskimos. Here the older men gathered together already in the autumn while the young men were out caribou hunting, and lived in autumn houses — qarmat — which they had built up on the sites of the old houses: and here they built snow houses in winter as soon as the snow became suitable for the purpose, here they had their dancing and festival house — qagi; some Eskimos are still alive who have had qarmat at Quilalukan. In summer too, Quilalukan was often inhabited; but since the trading station was built no one has lived there.*

I never tired of going there, at all hours of day or night, filming the sandpipers from empty nest to the clutch of eggs, to the day when six tiny chicks like feathered Ping-Pong balls ran hither and yon among the heather on toothpick legs, their frantic parents trying to marshal them into some kind of order; or spending hours in one of the ruined circles of the Thule dwellings on the banks of the river, lying in wait with the camera at the end of a lemming run, trying to get a whisker-to-nose closeup.

At first there was no one there; then, when the salmon run started, the men from the village would make their way along the beach or over the ice in the evening to fish until the early hours, standing on a gravel spit to cast out into the river before it disappeared under the icepans, the estuary loud with the screams of quarreling gulls, and Quilalukan alive again. Joshua, Jootanee and Levi and other little boys often came too, jigging for fish through holes in the ice with short poles and lengths of line, at once absorbed, then easily distracted as little boys the world over. Their Thule ancestors, whose house foundations lay nearby, would have understood perfectly.

I often took refuge from the wind in those circular hollows, where I entertained myself with speculations on their ancient inhabitants, and on the occupants of the two lonely gravesites close by, Hector Pitchforth and Robert Janes. And during the winter separating my two summers in Pond, I was able to find out a little more of their lives from the few books in my local library, and then, later, through the courtesy of the Royal Ca-

* *The Report of the Fifth Thule Expedition, 1921–24,* under Knud Rasmussen (Copenhagen: Flyndalske Boghaindeln, 1928), Vol. IV, *Archaeology of the Central Eskimos* by Therkel Mathiassen, p. 136.

nadian Mounted Police, from their photostatted official archives of the trial of Nokudlo, Janes's murderer.

Hector Pitchforth was the more difficult. He seems to have been one of those lonely enigmas, so often English, who turn their backs on their own country to seek out the anonymity of northern solitudes, and it was as though he were still resisting any attempts to break down this reserve.

What was known for certain was that he had been a commander in the Royal Navy during the 1914–1918 war, and that soon after that he had made his way out to the Arctic, becoming a trader at Home Bay, on the northeast coast of Baffin, on Davis Strait, for the same Sabellum Trading Company which had once had a post at Pond. He was to be the last employee of this company in the north.

Some time after arriving at Home Bay he reestablished the trading post as far away as possible from the Eskimo community, situating the shack which was both trading post and home on the point of Tikkegat. The shack was ten by fourteen feet, moss-chinked, so low that it was impossible to stand upright, with one small window to the west for light, plus two small pieces of glass in the south wall. Here he lived entirely alone, unvisited save by trading Eskimos, gaining yearly by his aloofness the reputation of being an eccentric, poring over the large collection of maps which was apparently his only interest. Toward the end of his life not even the Eskimos came near, for by now his acceptable eccentricity had changed to seeming madness, and they were afraid of him, as he would erupt out of the shack if anyone drew near, shouting wildly and even firing off a shotgun.

The last time he was seen alive by a white man was when Dr. Leslie Livingstone, the doctor who covered large areas of the eastern Arctic by dog team and boat from his practice at

Pangnirtung, visited Home Bay in 1924. He then saw Pitch-forth in a whaler with ten Eskimos, and, recalling the visit after Pitchforth's death, wrote that he then "seemed sane, but quite deaf, and his eyesight was poor."

Three years after Livingstone's visit the Hudson Bay manager at Clyde Bay, suspecting Pitchforth's death from reports received from Eskimos, sent word to the RCMP. A Constable Troup was dispatched with a dog team from Pond Inlet, arriving at Home Bay on April 14. He found a neglected shack, and forced open the doors "all snibbed from within," as he said in his report (he must have been Scottish). Lying on the bed, giving "every appearance of having died peacefully" was Pitch-forth. Constable Troup, having no available wood, sewed him up in three blankets, loaded him onto the sled and brought him back to Pond Inlet, where he probably performed a rough autopsy, as I heard it said in Pond that the cause of death was thought to be peritonitis.

Shortly afterward, Livingstone, on a dog team journey, having also heard of the suspected death from some Eskimos at Kiveetoo (the efficacy of the "bush telegraph" in the Arctic has always been one of its more remarkable aspects), went to Home Bay to ensure that the body had been removed. He gave a fairly detailed description of the shack, with its litter of cloth-ing and food and the impression of utter loneliness, finding it "one of the most pathetic scenes; one cannot imagine what it must have been for this man to have lived alone all these years." There was a good stock of food, guns and ammunition. "Not an Eskimo would come near him; but said that he was crazy and they were afraid of him."

(This fear, then, must have developed in the preceding three years, for there were certainly ten Eskimos, presumably una-fraid, with him in the whaler when Livingstone last saw him.)

It seemed to me, piecing together these various fragments,

that Pitchforth's behavior toward the end may not have been pure craziness, but that by now totally deaf and possibly blind — with his eccentricity developed into a more positive form — he began to behave as almost anyone living in a silent dark world would: to imagine he heard things, or sensed them, and therefore to live in constant fear of the unknown: starting up and suddenly firing his gun outside, shouting, to ward off intruders that he had no way of knowing were *not* there. This behavior would naturally be interpreted by would-be visiting Eskimos as thoroughly antagonistic, and in the end none would risk going near this armed, seemingly crazy man (in point of fact, no *loaded* guns were afterward found in the shack), and so they avoided the place altogether. Toward the end, if he *did* die of peritonitis, possibly the firing and shouting may have been a desperate attempt to draw attention to his plight.

Whatever the reason, whatever the truth behind his behavior, it seemed to me a sad, lonely little story, and I thought that that was the end of it.

And so it was, as far as actual proven fact went, but while tracking down the turbulent Mr. Janes I came across another reference to the trading post at Home Bay, which offered the possibility of another explanation.

This was in part of the RCMP archives of 1921, and it was a brief reference to the forthcoming investigation of another Arctic murder besides that of Janes: that of "An Eskimo in charge of the Sabellum Trading Company's outpost at Kiveetung, Home Bay." The murdered Eskimo, therefore, must have been Hector Pitchforth's immediate predecessor at Home Bay.

The Eskimo was

"stated to have become insane, claiming to be Christ. Acting under his order another Eskimo shot and killed two other natives who refused to accept the insane man's views or biddings. Some time later when the insane man was said to be threatening to kill a woman who

was on her knees at the time, a native named Kidlappick shot and
killed him when he was about to strike and kill the kneeling woman
with a hammer. Some time prior to this the insane man had been shot
and wounded by another or the same man, on account of his terroriz-
ing the community. The Eskimos on this occasion nursed his wound
until he became well, and it was after this that the murder took
place.

The account particularly interested me because it was obviously a case of "pibluktu"; and by a curious coincidence I had
just heard a fascinating and plausible environmental explanation for this so-called hysterical "possessed" condition, which
has cropped up from time to time among the Eskimos. There
are plenty of examples in Arctic literature, today, and two hundred years ago. The incidence among women is the highest, but
there have been plenty of men who first showed signs of withdrawal and suspicion, suspicion which erupted into violence;
they were then subjugated by their fellows until the symptoms
had passed. With women it more often took the form of imagining that they had been "taken over" — either bewitched or because they had sinned (by theft or something that hurt the
structure of day-to-day living in a close band) — and their actions too were often violent, if not against others against themselves. (There was a notorious case within the last few years of
a messianic woman leading her naked followers to their death
on the ice in winter.) Dogs, too, were often affected, showing,
except for the hydrophobia, all the signs of rabies. At these
times, they were, not unnaturally, shot by the white man. In
fact, at the time Dr. Livingstone was making his rounds toward
Home Bay, the year that Pitchforth died, he had to shoot several
of his dogs because of "rabies." That shrewd observer of the
pre-1914 scene, Alfred Tremblay, has this to say on the subject:

The adult Eskimo are often subject to a peculiar nervous affection, a
form of hysteria, which they call *pibluktu*. It seems to result from

the morbid brooding over absent or dead friends and relatives or a
fear of the future. The woman suffers most from it, and when
attacked with this form of hysteria, they will begin to scream and tear
off their clothes and run about screaming and gesticulating like someone possessed. They will rush out of the igloo in the coldest of
weather and run about, almost nude on the snow and ice until they
are exhausted. If the other Eskimo did not forcibly bring them back
they would certainly be frozen to death. The attack usually ends in a
fit of weeping and then the patient quietens down, the eyes are blood-
shot, the pulse high, and the whole body trembles for an hour or so
afterwards. Eskimo dogs and foxes also suffer from *pibluktu* and
although the symptoms seem to resemble those of hydrophobia, it
does not seem so dangerous or infectious. The dogs are generally shot.
Several Eskimos at Pond Inlet nearly lost all their dogs from this
disease.*

It was particularly fascinating to learn, soon after I read this,
that there could be a perfectly ordinary physical reason for
pibluktu, to cover both human and animal symptoms; a reason
so beautifully simple that — like all beautifully simple reasons
— one wonders why it has not been obvious before, or why no
basic folklore type of preventative had evolved over the centuries. Briefly — and unscientifically — the possible reason put
forward recently is that the symptoms could arise from the lack
of certain trace elements — copper, manganese, or cobalt — in the
diet of the affected. This could come about by a complex chance
cycle — given the right time in the right place in a train of
events, such as weather or geological conditions or marine
changes, affecting the minutiae of a fish's intake of food, resulting in a nutritional change to the eventual consumer of the fish
— either directly, or further among the line, as a seal which has
swallowed the fish and in turn been eaten by the Eskimo (or
dog or fox). Given at the same time the particular set of what

---

* Alfred Tremblay, *The Cruise of the Minnie Maud* (Quebec: Arctic
Exchange and Publishing Co., 1921).

I can only think of as internal mechanics (a good safe layman's phrase) to deal, or not deal, with this new development (biochemically, or what have you), and there you have the answer to apparent random selection in the victims. Very satisfying, if and when this piece of pathological detective work is proved. Like fitting in the last piece of a jigsaw puzzle.

So I have wondered ever since about poor, lonely, enigmatic Hector Pitchforth: it seems curious that so much mayhem occurred in such a tiny settlement as Home Bay; strange that Pitchforth's pattern of living degenerated into symptoms so like those of pibluktu victims — of his predecessor in fact — the increasing withdrawal, the aggression. For all we know, perhaps the white man who comes to live in the Arctic may be as susceptible to trace element deficiency as the natives, but because we tend to rationalize odd behavior by white standards, the physical cause goes undetected.

Of the trader Robert Janes, who had been a cause célèbre, I already knew a little. According to the Pond Inlet version, the Eskimos who had chosen Nokudlo to murder him had reason indeed. Not only had Janes given nothing in return for the skins brought to him, but he had turned dangerous and aggressive, threatening to shoot their dogs when pressed for trading goods, and even trying to abduct Nokudlo's wife Atagootsiak. When the law had eventually caught up with their deed, the Eskimos were astonished to be told they had done wrong, instead of being commended for having rid the community of a dangerous menace. Nokudlo's misdeed was made the occasion for a full-scale trial at Pond Inlet, at which he was found guilty and sentenced to ten years' imprisonment in the penitentiary in Manitoba.

Now, working in the library during the winter, I found my first mention of Robert Janes in a list of expeditions to the Canadian Arctic, where he appears as "an officer, from New-

foundland," aboard the C.G.S. *Arctic*, under the command of
Captain Bernier. This expedition took place in 1910–1911 with
the object of traversing McClure Strait. It was Bernier's third
expedition of the many which he made, and during which
much of Canada's Arctic territory was claimed officially.

Bernier's fourth expedition in 1912 is listed as having "the
object to look for gold reported by R. Janes in previous expedition." It seems that Janes had given out that "following information from an Eskimo," he had discovered gold nuggets in the
bed of the Esduron River on Eclipse Sound (Quilalukan). This
time the ship was the *Minnie Maud*, a two-masted schooner.
The redoubtable Alfred Tremblay was also on board.

Two other ships sailed at the same time in July in quest of the
gold, as an account of Janes's discovery had appeared in the
press early that year: the *Neptune* and the *Algernine*. The
Algernine was nipped in the ice outside Erik's Harbor and sank
within twenty minutes; the crew came ashore at Button Point,
then made their way to the government cache of provisions at
Albert Harbor. There they were picked up by the *Neptune* two
weeks later, and all proceeded to the Salmon River. Prospectors
were sent ashore, but only seams of coal were found after the
river had been panned for gold to its source. They reported
that the whole thing must have been either a deliberate hoax
or, more charitably, that Janes had been deluded.

Then the *Minnie Maud* investigated the river, including the
rocks and streams of the adjacent country in the search, but
found nothing. The *Minnie Maud* also wintered at Pond, while
Alfred Tremblay set off on yet another of his remarkable jour-
neys by dog sled.

There is no mention of Janes's whereabouts at this time. However, he had returned to the area (possibly still believing in his
own story, hoping for further information from the Eskimos?)
and set up as a trader on the Patricia River about thirty-five

miles from Pond, by 1916. Here things went from bad to worse
with him: summers came and went and still the supply ship
with the necessary trading goods aboard did not arrive; his
financial backing from Newfoundland fell through, and consequently the Eskimos refused to bring any more furs. "It is stated
that disputes arose between him and sundry Eskimos over
financial matters."

Nokudlo was one of the sundry Eskimos. Finally Janes threw
in the sponge. "His circumstances during the last year and a half
of his life are described as having been very miserable. In 1919
he made efforts to obtain a passage to St. John's, but these were
frustrated . . . he decided to make his way to Chesterfield. . . ."

Chesterfield was on Hudson Bay, a long and terrible journey
by dog team down the west coast of Baffin and across the
Melville peninsula. En route Janes arrived at Cape Crawford on
March 14, where there was a small Eskimo settlement, and
where he was again to meet Nokudlo. Soon after arriving, he
had another dispute with the Eskimos:

He had been very angry and had threatened to shoot their dogs and
to shoot some of them. The details of the killing . . . were that Janes
was in an igloo, when in accordance with a preconcerted plan
Oorooreungnak entered and told him that another Eskimo had some
skins which he was willing to sell; Janes (who was very eager to
obtain furs) came out, and on his emerging Nokudlo shot him
through the body. The unfortunate man did not fall immediately, and
Ahteetah went up to him and pushed him down; Nokudlo fired again,
the bullet going through his head and killing him. Evidence was given
that one or more general discussions were held at which the decision
to kill Janes was taken. The Eskimos insisted that they were greatly
in fear of Janes. After the murder had taken place, a number of
Eskimos gave the murdered skins as a reward.

(Thus, although there could be no doubt that it was a pre-
conceived murder from the point of view of white justice, it was

entirely within the framework of custom and common sense
that had evolved of necessity among the Eskimos: those who
endangered the security or survival of the band — as with the
Home Bay murder of the insane dangerous man — should not
be allowed to do so. However, individual opinion as to who
could be considered bad or dangerous enough to deserve death
might be prejudicial; therefore the responsibility of individual
action was eliminated by a conference among other responsible
men in the band. A very sensible arrangement. "Such executions
for the peace of the community," Peary remarks, "were rare
however"; more usually the menace to the community was re-
strained by his fellows until such time as he recovered his balance — again as the Eskimos nursed the crazed man's wounds
at Home Bay, where, however, restraint had not had any thera-
peutic effect.)

When word of the murder trickled down to Ottawa, a Sergeant Joy of the RCMP was sent to investigate, being invested
with the additional powers of magistrate and coroner so that he
could hold an inquest. Fortunately the Hudson Bay Company
was setting up a post for the first time at Pond Inlet, so he was
able to make the long journey in their company ship, the
Nascopie.

When Sergeant Joy eventually arrived by dog team at the
scene of the crime, neither Nokudlo, Ahteetah Ooroooreung-
nak were there any longer. However, the other men of the band
welcomed Joy and led him cheerfully to the place where they
had interred Janes's body beneath the snow, undoubtedly feeling rather pleased with themselves, for burial was not Eskimo
custom, but "these men knowing that the practice among white
men is different, went to considerable trouble to inter him."
("An admirable and Christian act," observed Sergeant Joy
approvingly.) They must have been very surprised to learn
that far from patting them on the back the arm of the law pro-

posed to take them back to Pond Inlet along with Janes's body as material witnesses at an inquest: apparently in the white man's eyes a Very Serious Crime indeed had been committed. However, obliging as ever, eight witnesses rounded up their families and dogs and returned with Sergeant Joy.

Back at Pond, in his role of coroner, Joy conducted an autopsy and held an inquest, the verdict being that "Nokudlo did feloniously and of his malice aforethought kill and murder the said Robert Janes by shooting him through the body and head with a rifle, from which he instantly died.

"And so do further say that Oorooreungnak and Ahteetah did feloniously and of their malice aforethought aid and abet the same Nokudlo." Then, changing into the role of magistrate, he issued warrants for the arrest of the three men, and later conducted a preliminary inquiry when they were committed for trial.

But before this, Sergeant Joy had to round his prisoners up, which was quite a job:

The rest of the winter and spring were occupied in collecting the three men for whom the warrants were out, as well as the necessary witnesses; these people were scattered all over the northern part of Baffin Island, an area of some three hundred miles long by two hundred miles wide, and to the usual difficulties of travel in this inhospitable region was added a scarcity of dogs, due to an epidemic which prevailed. [Then — a very nice touch to the methods of getting your man in the Arctic:] Staff Sergeant Joy sent messages to these people to come to him, giving assistance in the way of provisions when necessary and one by one the persons incriminated and most of the witnesses made their appearance at the post.

When all had appeared, plus the entire family entourage of each, which included at least a hundred dogs, the capacity of the region around Pond to support the hunters was strained to its limits:

During 1923 a court will be sent to Pond Inlet and the accused will
be tried. They are now in the vicinity, under open arrest. A feature
of the situation is that it is necessary to provide for the prisoners and
witnesses and their families, the detention interfering with their customary habits of life, and the vicinity of Pond Inlet being unable to
support so considerable a number of people. The confinement to one
locality and the anxiety have told severely on the prisoners.

(The Eskimo must have thought the ways of the white man
more than passing strange: who, in their right senses, would
insist that hunters hunt in an overhunted area with the whole
of the eastern Arctic available?)

Now the powers that be, probably spurred on as well by the
persistence of Janes's father, who appears to have been an influ-
ential man, decided that this would be an opportune time to
show the might of government in the very young Northwest
Territories, to make the people there feel that they were well
and truly a part of Canada now, and to get the message home
to the natives that law and order were there to stay, whether
concerning murder, trapping out of season or not filling in tax
forms — and that those who did not observe the laws would be
punished.

Consequently a full judicial court, to be conducted "with all
the panoply and decorum of a Supreme Court in civilization"
(i.e., complete with wigs and robes; counsels for the crown,
counsels for the defense; scarlet-coated mounties as prisoners'
escorts, and judge's orderlies), was shipped off to Pond Inlet
in the S.S. *Arctic* — the most northerly full-scale trial ever held.

A jury was selected from the officers and crew of the *Arctic*,
and the trial was held at the RCMP post. (I wonder how on
earth they all fitted in.) Nokudlo was convicted of man-
slaughter, and sentenced to ten years at Stoney Mountain Penitentiary. Oorooreungnak received two years' imprisonment with
hard labor to be served at Pond Inlet. (His family and dogs of

course moved in with him, and helped lay out the boulders around the new RCMP post; when he went off hunting to support them, they cheerfully took up the whitewash brush where he had left off.) Ahteetah was acquitted.

After the termination of the trial, the judge addressed the entire Eskimo population outside the detachment, telling what they had to expect from the representatives of the Government, that they could expect kindness and protection from the police if they behaved well, but if they committed any crime they could expect to be punished.

They all immediately afterwards joined in three generous cheers for the judge.

This was less than fifty years ago, yet even in that time how absurdly complacent and pompous does the word "generous" strike one nowadays: a group of Eskimos, of whom it is probable that not one among them knew what he was cheering or why, but, polite to a man, repeating like dutiful parrots the strange phrase "Hip, Hip, Hooray" to a stranger who promised them not only kindness and protection (from what? — alas, not the further encroachment of the white man), but punishment if they did not forsake this foolish notion that their own laws had worked very nicely thank you for the last few thousand years, and step smartly into twentieth-century legal discipline — and all, lucky people, for the privilege of continuing to live in their own country.

"The effects of the sentence," said the judge, "I believe will have a more beneficial effect than a sentence of death. The prisoner Nokudlo was led away immediately after sentence was passed to the ship, through a gazing crowd of his own people. It is hardly possible that a native . . . could have been subjected to a greater humiliation than to be led away directly under the eyes of not less than a hundred of his relatives and friends."

But the learned judge was presupposing the emotions of a

hundred white relatives and friends of convicted prisoners in white civilization. In Pond Inlet a hundred relatives and friends saw a beaming Nokudlo boarding a nice big ship to sail off with these unaccountable white strangers who had arrived to say that he was a Very Bad Man indeed — and then took him back to live with them, and to be housed, clothed and fed at their own expense. Such hospitality was truly remarkable.

I have seen a photograph of Nokudlo at this time, taken on board the *Arctic*, grinning like a delighted Cheshire cat.

He was not to enjoy ten years' unlimited hospitality, however. He contracted tuberculosis at Stoney Mountain and was returned to Pond a year later, dying shortly afterward; it was then assumed by the bewildered one hundred that he had somehow offended his hosts and been driven out.

Hearsay has it that only the representatives of law and order were satisfied with the verdict, the general consensus of private white opinion being that frankly Janes was a thoroughly undesirable, upsetting character in the Arctic, and that if anyone was a Bad Man it was he — that the three rousing cheers should have been for Nokudlo, if anyone, for getting rid of him. And this idea persists today.

That was the impression I had too, when I had finished reading the various reports. Then I happened to be reading Alfred Tremblay's accounts of some of his sledging expeditions undertaken in 1912, after the abortive gold search, with particular interest in the ones made around the north Baffin area, as many of the places I had been to or flown over were mentioned, when suddenly I saw Nokudlo's name again. And after that my eyes were opened somewhat.

Nokudlo had appeared in Igloolik this time (he certainly got around) shortly after Tremblay arrived there. Tremblay was on his way back to join Captain Bernier at Pond Inlet, intending to explore parts of the Foxe Channel on the way, with the assistance of the Igloolik natives who knew that terrain. But suddenly and inexplicably their attitude to his plans altered: he could persuade no one to accompany him, being given nothing but obvious lies for the refusal. He decided to compromise, and make instead a flying visit to look at the quartz veins on Melville Sound. Again he received no cooperation: no one would accompany him. Finally, and only by a ruse, he persuaded Takkowah, the young son of Eetooksardjooiah, to accompany him to the quartz veins.

It was only afterward that Tremblay found out why the normally helpful Eskimos of Igloolik had refused to accompany him on either this or his other projected expeditions: Nokudlo had wanted to go directly to Pond, and had been quite cunning in his attempts to stop Tremblay going elsewhere with anyone else: "Nokudlo, by his underground work, and which was unknown to me at the time, had frightened the natives of Igloolik from accompanying me. . . ."

On his return from Melville Peninsula with Takkowah, Tremblay duly set out for Pond on April 15, 1913, but was determined to go by way of Cockburn Land, instead of the usual Scheming and Admiralty Sound way. Nokudlo and his twelve dogs were with the party, the arrangement being that he should accompany it as far as Milne Inlet at least, as he was the only Eskimo who knew this overland route.

A few days later Tremblay was to write in his journal: "A disagreeable incident happened in the igloo which might easily have resulted in bloodshed, owing to the lies and underhand work of Nokudlo. . . ."

The trouble, briefly summarized from a lengthy description, was this: young Takkowah had set off ahead of the party for Pond Inlet as his father, Eetooksardjooiah, had commissioned him to buy a rifle and ammunition there, then return with them to Igloolik. Takkowah had fifteen foxskins for the rifle's purchase, and some walrus tusks for the ammunition. Tremblay doubted that the tusks would fetch much ammunition, so he lent six additional foxskins. Eetooksardjooiah agreed to repay this debt at Murray Maxwell Bay, where Tremblay would be camped for ten days of seal hunting prior to the overland journey across Cockburn Land.

On April 21 Nokudlo said that he was going to leave the party and follow Takkowah to Pond Inlet. Tremblay said No very firmly to that idea: he was the only one who knew the route; he must remain, and furthermore remain with the party until the agreed rendezvous with Eetooksardjooiah.

Nokudlo then told me that Eetooksardjooiah was not going to bring the foxskins and had told him (Nokudlo) that I was of no account, that only Captain Bernier was of any account and that he had no intention of following after me. When Nokudlo told me this I became very angry, as I was sure that he was lying to me, and if I had had enough seal meat, would have forced him to return with me to confront Eetooksardjooiah. Had I done so, there would assuredly have been a fight with a probable certainty of bloodshed. I told the Eskimos that a white man was not going to be cheated after having done a kindness and said that unless one of them started immediately to overtake Takkowah, and bring back the letter (a letter he had written to Bernier, authorizing goods to be handed over to Takkowah) and the foxskins that I had given him, I would take them all back to Igloolik and confront Eetooksardjooiah and get at the truth of the story. At this they became alarmed and Nokudlo became very pale. They begged me not to go back to Igloolik. . . .

On May 8, Tremblay met young Takkowah in Milne Inlet, returning from his mission: ". . . he confirmed that Eetooksardjooiah had never spoken in the manner indicated by Nokudlo, and that he intended to bring me the foxskins."

Nokudlo in the meantime, fearing Tremblay's wrath when he heard the truth about his underhanded goings-on from Takkowah, whipped up his dogs and made a swift departure, reaching Pond long before the party, then immediately taking off for the comparative obscurity of Button Point.

Tremblay finished his account:

From the moment that Nokudlo arrived at Igloolik, I had trouble with the natives, who, from being willing and anxious to accompany and assist me in every way, suddenly became sullen and suspicious, and refused to accompany or help in any way.

Nokudlo, therefore, had the dubious honor of being the only Eskimo in Alfred Tremblay's eighteen years of living and traveling with the Eskimos who stirred him to anger. In fact he was the only one who even received a derogatory word, for Tremblay had nothing but admiration and respect for these people, and a true humility: "There are few things that the Eskimos require to learn from the white man, but there are many Christian qualities inherent in the Eskimos that the white man, on his present plane of civilisation, might copy and practise with a resultant benefit to the peace and happiness of the world."

So much for this Nokudlo, the devious, the rabblerouser; a somewhat different image to the uncomprehending aboriginal victim of civilization and law nine years later. We know from Tremblay's account that he was in the area when Bernier returned to look "for gold reported by R. Janes in previous expeditions, following information given him from an Eskimo." One is left with the irresistible conjecture as to what part he played in that, whether "the Eskimo" might have been Nokudlo himself.

❧ *Chapter 7* ❧

Just before we left the first year there had been great excitement at Pond: Joshua, a young Eskimo returning from hunting, had brought Father Mary a complete Dorset-era wooden mask and a few other artifacts which he had found at Button Point, suddenly exposed by the crumbling away of a bank of sod after possibly nearly a thousand years of burial. "The greatest archaeological find in the Arctic," said Father Mary, excited as a little boy, for up to now only fragments of such masks had been found.

It was in a wonderful state of preservation: a warm reddy-brown, stained by iron oxide probably, incised around the chin and cheeks in a tattoo pattern, with slits for the eyes, and small square even teeth carved into the mouth opening. There was still a fragment of what looked like a knot of hair on the rim of the forehead, and indications that there might have been hair on the upper lip too. Tentative archaeological opinion is that such masks were probably part of an Angakkoq's — or sorcerer's — stock in trade. After we had all photographed, sketched and exclaimed over it, it was to be dispatched to the museum at Ottawa.

Father Mary could not take off for Button Point immediately, as he obviously longed to do, for not only were the ice conditions now impossible, but he was just on the point of leaving for his late summer dig at Kiluktoo, about seventy miles away on Navy Board Inlet. Whatever else might still be in situ in the newly exposed cliff edge would have to wait until next year — a real cliffhanger, in fact, and never suspended at a more tantalizing to-be-continued point.

Back in civilization I often thought about the mask — and even saw it again: in the pages of the *National Geographic* magazine, accompanying an article by Father Mary on his life with the Eskimos. That, and the fact that I recognized so many of the faces in the superb color photographs accompanying the article, made me more than ever eager to get back to Pond Inlet to hear the next installment of The Mask. I had learned by now that the pre-Dorset people were the earliest known migrants from the west, and made their appearance in Baffin around 2000 B.C. By about 800 B.C. they had evolved into the Dorset people, who were the originators of snowhouses, or igloos. But by A.D. 900 they seem to have vanished, or were overtaken by the first wave of the Thule people as they followed the coast eastward from Alaska, a people of an entirely different culture, and from whom all present Eskimos are descended. With a few very scattered exceptions, the only existent wooden artifacts of the Dorset culture have been excavated at Button Point.

So it was the most exciting news of all to hear from John Scullion, moments after the plane had touched down the following spring, that instead of hearing the second installment I would actually be there on the cliff: we were to accompany him and Father Mary on a trip that would handily combine government inspection with an archaeological dig at Button Point.

Furthermore we would be traveling with two dog teams, one of which would remain with Father Mary at Button Point, and I could, if I liked, stay on there until he returned.

If I liked . . . I didn't come down to earth for the next three days, until I was actually sitting on the komatik, with a borrowed tent under the caribou skins, and the camera batteries once more grinding into my hips.

The expedition had grown by this time to three dog teams and to include young Susie Scullion, aged ten, her Eskimo friend, Katerina, and a photographer, Eberhard Otto, who had suddenly turned up on an assignment from *Arts Canada*. Besides all his other cameras, Eberhard planned on using an enormous professional affair — the kind that is mounted on a tripod and requires the disappearance of its owner behind a black cloth, and a dark room wherein to change the plates every ten exposures. Dark rooms being at a premium on such a trip, he had brought his own along with him — a large plastic garbage bin. Into this Eberhard proposed to insert as much of his six feet five inches as possible; over what remained outside we were to draw up his sleeping bag and secure it around the bin. It sounded interesting. We could hardly wait to try it out. In the meantime the bin, lashed onto the end of the komatik, made a very comfortable back rest.

Eberhard and John were with Joatanee, who had twelve dogs to his team; Father Mary and the girls were with Jobee, with fifteen dogs; while Susan and I were with Oodlateetah, who looked about fourteen, but turned out to be seventeen, and very competent. We had ten dogs, plus a young follower who was either an apprentice or just along for the trip.

Once we were on our way with the three teams fanned out one behind the other and had settled in to the feel of the komatik again, it was sheer quiet bliss compared to the noise and lurchings of being towed by a skidoo — all the difference, in fact, between being under sail or engine. Also, with only two of us aboard this time there was room to change position. At first, in the shelter of Pond Bay, it was warm in the brilliant sun, but later as Mount Herodier was rounded we pulled on every available extra. "Woy, woy," Oodlateetah called softly sometimes, and the lead dog would bear off to the right, while something that sounded like "Aie-aie" was the left turn signal. Sometimes he jumped off and ran to the flank of the team, cracking and flicking with his whip for encouragement; sometimes he jogged alongside the komatik to warm up. Occasionally, on a flat, unwatery expanse we followed his example, but it was difficult to manage more than a hundred feet or so at a time, with bulky clothing and boots sinking in the snow, before making a thankful sideways leap back on.

I don't know which is best — the wonderment of first experience, never knowing what lies around the corner, the sharpness of impression. Or the return, recognizing, comparing, remembering — there was our campsite at Kuktiyuk rolling slowly past, the same red oil drum on the beach, places where I had walked; I was seeing this time, not just another river rushing white over glacial boulders, but the river beside which I had sat watching Bunnee carve the polar bear. Even particular rock formations I remembered, shapes of boulders fallen and frozen into the ice; the very place where we stopped to make tea on the freezing return from the floe edge last year; and there, where the skidoo broke down going through the water. . . .

Always there were the fascinating long humps of our three shadows traveling with us, sometimes gliding over the snow, sometimes mirrored along with the mountains in the blue water lying over the ice. And when I turned my back on them it was to watch the other komatiks running against the sun, the black silhouetted shapes, the legs of the dogs trotting close in step, like a centipede, their shadows long and reaching out toward

me. Closer they looked less romantic: John like a burly Santa
Claus without the beard, in contrast to Eberhard's thin length;
Father Mary sitting neatly sidesaddle on the rear of his komatik, the two giggling, jumping-on-and-off little girls between him
and Jobee, who could not have been more than four feet, six
inches tall, if that, and had a dark round old face, just like a
troglodyte. A short pipe stuck in his mouth was almost as much
a feature of his face as his nose. Susan and I must have presented an interesting silhouette to them too: slight, thin
Oodlateetah, bulky us, and the outsize garbage bin. We must
have looked like dowager Daughters of the Empire off on an
antipollution campaign.

We swished along under the towering cliffs of Beloeil, hearing Oodlateetah's "woy, woys" and "aie-aies" and the occasional yelp of a dog thrown back in the faintest echo. Far far
up beyond the pinnacles, the sky was empty and cloudless as
my mind as the hours passed, incapable of registering any
thought more profound than "that is a paw print, that is water,
blue, white, etc."

Sometimes one of the other teams drew level, and then we
would bow ceremoniously to one another as we ran alongside.
Then the panting mouths of their dogs were on a level with my
knees, and lying like an outrigger across the komatik I could
film from only a few inches away. Joatanee's lead was a thin
slight bitch, much of the hair rubbed off at her shoulders. She
fascinated me, the intense pointed face, eyes fixed straight
ahead even when she passed so close to mine, the taut trace.

Eskimo dogs mainly pull their loads widespread, unlike the
single file of Indian dogs necessitated by narrow trails and for-
ests. The fan of the traces, attached to a canvas shoulder
harness which extends to the withers, comes together about
eight feet before the runners of the komatik, where the individual bone rings of the traces form a tight cluster, then continue

in a single rope of thick intertwined sealskin; ookjuk, the bearded seal, makes exceptionally strong strips of hide. The lead dog, and the second — which usually runs close and to his left — take the brunt of the strain, which is then apportioned out through the fan. Traces — depending on the team and the skill of the driver — tangle hopelessly if there is much changing of position, and usually have to be sorted out every two hours. The lash of the driver's whip must be about thirty feet long, and when not in use trails along far behind the komatik, the tip wiggling along like a fast little snake. Sometimes when Oodlateetah saw a slack trace, or a dog changed position, he stood up on the runners; his arm moved back so that the lash curled alongside us, then forward with a crack, and the tip would flick with unerring accuracy across the hindquarters of the miscreant. Instantly, to an anguished howl, the komatik leaped forward. Very often the anguished howl came long before the lash touched, or when, rarely, Oodlateetah missed because his victim had dodged back in among his fellows in time. Our lead dog pulled steadily, trotting along for hour after hour; the second, a big black dog, ran with the off and near legs working together, in a kind of roll. The going was heavy for them, with the snow slushy and slow, and wide areas of surface water.

By the first tea stop, many of the dogs were limping badly or going on three paws, the snow imprinted in scarlet patterns after their passing. Sealskin boots were cut for them now, slitted for the claws, and bound with thongs. Soon after leaving Pond, a big husky had appeared and fallen into place beside our second dog, so alike that they must have been siblings; but he was very lame and soon dropped behind. Now as we drank our tea he came into view again; he had only time for a brief lie down among the team before we were off again, and he started up wearily to follow. Far behind him I could just make

out with the glasses another dog, and began to understand the
why and wherefore of the coming of that dog on Bylot.

My understanding was made even clearer hours later when
the dog on the far right flank collapsed. It had been dragging
more and more, and suddenly just keeled over to be dragged
along the ice by the team. Oodlateetah halted, and went over
to the dog, who lay on its side, eyes open, quite still. He kicked
it (though not hard), then lifted it by the scruff of the neck to
set it on its feet, but the dog just fell limply back. Oodlateetah
cut the trace loose, got back on the komatik, and we started
off again, the dog's eyes still open and blank. I watched as long
as I could through the glasses, but there was no movement. The
others, used to this, said that probably it would lie there for a
few hours, then follow our tracks — if its heart hadn't given
out.

Some time later the passing scene was enlivened when young
Susie miscalculated her jump back onto her komatik and fell
straight into a deep sheet of water. Like a good child who has
lived among the Eskimos, she managed to make a joke of it,
although her teeth were chattering and she must have been
frozen. We all contributed some dry clothing, but could only
produce moccasins for footwear; by the time we had topped
her off with my rubber smock, which came to her ankles, and
tied plastic bags over the moccasins to keep them dry, she
looked very odd indeed. The garbage bin now revealed its ver-
satility — we stowed the soaking clothes inside, and continued
on our way.

After twelve hours of traveling we were all pretty cold, and
our eventual destination, Kabloonavercortahlik, sighted from
four mist-shrouded promontories away, looked very bleak and
uninviting. This part of Baffin is nothing but a snowcap in the
interior, and the mountains on the shoreline are just the cut-off
end: steep white slopes, with only the sheer windswept cliffs

showing up black. Before we could reach the desolate little peninsula, a difficult buildup of ice entailed much shoving and hauling from all hands until we could reach the shoreline and the tired dogs lie down.

Our tent was pitched on a gravel platform above the boulder beach — and a cold and drafty tent it turned out to be, with no floor, and more suited for a July holiday in the Lake District. Father Mary's, a splendid nylon French affair consisting of a tent within a tent, rose on the ice, while John and the Eskimos settled for the beach. There was no sun, and even after all our exertions we felt chilled through to the bone. By 5 A.M., however, the soup-stew supper was going on the stove. We stood on the ice around the komatik and wolfed it down, then crawled as quickly as possible into sleeping bags to maintain the warmth produced by the refueling, wearing everything except parkas and boots. I looked out briefly to see the sun creeping round the headland as our lame follower crept into camp too and lay down with our team on the beach.

Kabloonavercortahlik means "White man here." The white man was still here — his bones resting beneath boulders on the hillside above, an unmarked cross preserving his anonymity, for no one seems to know who he was, only that he must have been very tall, as it is a long grave. There was a persistent rumor that he had been buried with considerable gold; an official inspection some years ago confirmed this: he had several gold fillings in his teeth. John walked up to see that the site was orderly; we tidied up a few boulders, then left him in lonely peace.

As on all these few-and-far-between peninsulas of this coast there was plenty of evidence of long habitation from Dorset times to today. I prodded around on an old campsite and found some flint chippings and a scraper almost immediately. Nearby there was the present-day wooden skeleton frame of a tent, and lying under the rocks a large stone cooking pot, belonging to a family that camped here while hunting — a vessel that would have fetched a hundred dollars or more in an Eskimo crafts shop, but which was safe here from light-handed tourists.

I did not like this place. When the sun went behind the mountain the cold crept as insidiously into bones as the mist encroached on the shore. The only thing to do was to keep moving. I walked around the point, close to the shore, past cave formations and huge boulders rolled down from the mountain above, until thankfully I found the sun again. I wanted to sit there by the river and thaw out, but looking back I could see the mist rolling up around the shore to the campsite, so I returned reluctantly, this time following the ice. It was eerie out there in the swirling mist, with the ice statues and silence, and I was glad to find some bootprints to follow around the cracks. I was gladder still to find back at the cold bleak camp that Father had decided that his test site held meager prospects for anything exciting, and that we would be pushing on the next day.

That must make it nighttime now, I decided, watchless as usual; and retired to the tent, where I encased the sleeping bag in garbage bags and had a good gulp of Mother McCree's Cough Syrup from the vinegar bottle for additional warmth; then, removing only my boots — and those with the greatest reluctance — I closed my eyes against the cold fingers of mist reaching through the tent flaps and sides, and went into brief hibernation until the spring hour of departure.

Someone said it was about noon when the camp stirred next day, so I don't know whether it was a very long or a very brief hibernation. Nor had I any idea what time it was when we left. Normally, I wrote things down at odd times of the day in a journal/sketchbook; but this seems to have been one of the few times when there was no entry beyond "Cold $+$ $+$ Cold . . .

bloody depressing place; ugh." I only remember now that it took a very long time to cross the twenty-five miles from coast to coast, with a great deal of open water navigation, and that Button Point seemed as endlessly far away for hours as it did the year before when I was heading for it. I think it must have been nine or ten at night when the team at last plodded wearily up the narrow channel beneath the rocks.

There they were staked out, and their boots removed. They had not been fed since we left two days before, and they were not fed now, although much later I saw Jobee cut up a small seal that the team had run down on the way and distribute it among his fifteen dogs.

On the grassy plateau above, we staked out the four tents haphazardly, according to the occupants' whim and the prevailing wind. Father Mary's tent was on the edge of the little cliff, almost above the excavation site. John's was within hailing distance; the Eskimos preferred a western exposure on one side of the peninsula; we preferred a southeastern one on the other, cannily situated near a nice ravine too.

A hundred yards or so back stood a solitary shed, nailed together from pieces of packing case, and it was in this that Father expected to house his magnificent new Portable Camper's Convenience — there was some speculation on what constituted a Portable Camper: infant Girl Guides? vacationing sedan chair users? — whose pristine white seat and collapsible RustPruf legs, designed to support a garbage bag, he had already put together, following the easy directions enclosed. But the hut floor was found to be about four feet deep in blubber, so he compromised with a fascinating new bow to the proprieties: like an outside throne the seat was flanked by oil barrels, two on either side, the hut wall at its back, but nothing in front, which commanded a magnificent view over the frozen bay, and was in turn commanded by all who passed before.

A few yards away was the shelter hut — a standard government one-window crackerbox type, the floor deep in cigarette butts, mud, grass, bones, fur, etc. There was an enormous sleeping platform at the far end, two bed frames, and the remains of two chairs, plus a stove. Hanging on a nail by the door was a beautiful caribou parka, a child's, brand new, which some wife must have been working on last week while the men were out hunting. There were two little fur pigtails at the end of the hood, and the whole was fringed with leather.

We swept out the floor with goose wings, and got the stove going with the help of some bits of blubber. There was a sack of spilled coal outside, from the Mary Lake coal seam, only about sixty miles from Pond: very soft coal, mostly dross, which makes a sulky fire with little heat, but which lasts an amazingly long time. Soon the hut was very snug — too snug almost, by the time eleven of us were crowding in eating John's stew du jour, into which Father dropped porridge oats, biscuits, etc., for thickening — an ancient Arctic culinary secret, he said. Five minutes after he had polished his bowl clean he was down at the site taking preliminary measurements.

Mathiassen* of Rasmussen's Danish Expedition, assisted by Peter Freuchen, made the first archaeological exploration of Button Point in 1923; the evidence of it was only a hundred yards from the present site, where Joshua had found the mask. He came, briskly put twenty Eskimos to work, and departed shortly afterward, having come to the conclusion that Button Point was unsatisfactory for any extensive excavation, the peculiarities of the strata reducing the value of uncovered artifacts to a kind of chronological bran pie. Forty-five years later, after three seasons' extensive exploration, excavation and testing,

---

* *The Report of the Fifth Thule Expedition, 1921–24*, under Knud Rasmussen. Vol. IV, *Archaeology of the Central Eskimos*, by Therkel Mathiassen), p. 136.

Father Mary concurred with Mathiassen's opinion, adding only the rider:

However, if the purpose is to collect archaeological specimens, there are certainly many more interesting ones to be found at Button Point. But it is noticeable that, next to areas with heavy concentration of artefacts, are other areas almost devoid of any cultural remains. It is almost as if most of the artefacts of interest lay in pockets . . . and it takes a very special archaeological nose to find these pockets!

Now, we hoped, his own professionally questing nose might follow the geological scent back from the position of the eroded turf on which the mask was found in the depths of the permafrost, and there locate a cache that would be of pre-Dorset cultural significance — a cache possibly of the accoutrements of a sorcerer.

It was not going to be an easy quest. The permafrost on the steep eroded face of the peninsula was the most frustrating of barriers: the turf had to be peeled and chipped away across the surface; then, when the ancient dark ice was exposed, layers of bones protruding from it or tantalizing shapes barely discernible captive within, work had to be suspended until the next few centimeters melted. The sun only struck directly on the site early in the morning: by nine o'clock or so it was glancing obliquely. There was an additional barrier to be overcome too, because the top level of bank had slipped down over the course of many years to form an overhanging buttress of solid ice stuffed with bones and stones before the proper chronological levels of the land behind. When one considers the very short season in which it is possible to work, archaeology in the high Arctic has incomparable difficulties. The only compensation is the state of perfect preservation in which the permafrost holds its secrets. Even the feathers of birds eaten a thousand years ago can still sometimes be identified.

When I looked down at the site that first morning, Father
Mary and John were hard at it with shovels and small picks, like
miners at a coal face, making the initial clearance, the accumulated loose earth and peat from the barren top level flying out
behind them and down the slope. Lazily, I left them to this
uninspiring, laborious stage. I wanted to explore beyond the
peninsula: there would be plenty of time for the site when the
others had gone.

The Button Point scene that morning remains indelibly
printed on memory. Silhouetted against the sky, Susan was
perched on a rock, sketching the laborers on the site below, the
ringing of pick and shovel against ice providing background
music. Below them again on the rocks, Jobee, his hands bloody,
was feeding his team — the disemboweled carcass spread-
eagled on the rocks — throwing chunks in turn at the eager
whining dogs, while, like a Greek chorus, the other two teams
stood singing enviously. Oodlateetah half knelt on a rock to the
right, a telescope to his eye. Beyond them on the ice intermit-
tent cracks rang out like pistol shots as Susie and Katerina practiced with dog whips. The figure of Joatanee, black against the
ice, appeared round the headland, carrying two buckets of
fresh water. All this against a fairy-tale background of little
icebergs, their shapes softened and changed minute to minute
by the soft white mist creeping around the point, and shot
through with random shafts of sunlight. And standing on the
hill behind, silhouetted surrealistically against the vast backdrop of the sky, was the positively Victorian watch-the-birdie
outline of Eberhard, his head and shoulders under the black
cloth of the camera, his long legs sticking out behind the three
of the tripod, like a five-footed predatory bird. And I sat
propped against a tent pole, writing in my journal, taping the
sounds, like some anthropologist from outer space recording the
cultural behavior of the Earth natives.

I took to the hills. There was no urgency of commitment for me; if I too had a thing to do in the next few days, an art to practice, it was to potter peacefully, with nothing particular in view, to absorb and be absorbed by my surroundings — a mindless art at which, along with beachcombing, I excel.

The base of the mountains rising steeply from the root of the peninsula could be reached by the plateau ridge that followed the coastline for miles, or by the longer way from the slopes of the river valley. I took the hard way the first time, not from masochism, but because I didn't know any better, scrambling endlessly over the great cascade of boulders at the base. Underneath was the sound of rushing water, even though the scree above, extending deep into a rift between the lower hills, was bone dry. At one point the clay had formed into a long hummock, rather like a manmade conduit, and here the water sounded hollow and melodious. I sat there for a long time, a Lapland longspur perched on a rock only a few feet away, trying to pick out with my knife the dark red rounded inserts, glinting like garnets, set into so many of the boulders. Soon the figures at the end of Button Point looked like ants, and by the time I heaved myself up to the top it was as though I had the world to myself. Behind, further mountain ranges stretched endlessly, and before me I could see the dark blue curving floe edge far out beyond the ice off the point, with here and there the geometrical patterns and colors of ice cracks and leads. Crawling over the ice, closer in, were two double-spaced black dots — Oodlateetah and Joatanee off to hunt seals. Twenty-five miles or more away the mountains behind Kabloonavercortahlik were mirrored perfectly in a great sheet of blue water. A pair of horned larks rose leisurely, but instead of ascending in the way one always associates with larks, they descended a few hundred feet down the mountain.

Looking across the whole sweep of Baffin Bay, I tried to

imagine Nokudlo whipping his dogs on across its expanse as he
fled to the point below me; the frozen, wet and miserable men
from the wrecked *Algernine* picking their way across the ice
floes to reach the rocks far down there. And then there was the
account old Ootoovah had given recently of being told by her
grandmother how in the whaling days the people of Pond used
to gather here in early August when the ice was breaking up to
watch for the first arrival of the whaling ships. Everyone —
men, women and children — up on the hills, with telescopes
trained on the horizon; then the feasting and the festivities
when the whalers finally — and it must have been dramatically
— appeared.. The first comers were here about 1810, and the
last was shortly before the 1914 war. The slaughter must have
been terrific, for the shores are littered with giant single bones
and vertebrae of bow, Greenland and blue whales. We had
passed one of the enormous iron cauldrons for rendering the
blubber on our way here, just a few miles down the coast.

There are pitifully few whales left nowadays. Even as far
back as 1906, Tremblay reported sighting only one Greenland
or right whale, and it is a pity that no one heeded the words of
his report: "The Governments of Canada and Denmark would
do well to prohibit the further killing of these valuable and interesting sea-mammals for a period of twenty years, or the race
of whales will soon become extinct."

On my way down I was bending to pick up a fox skull when
a hare started up almost at my feet. I had seen them in the distance only and had not expected them to be so large. I watched
him for several minutes, snow white and beautiful, lolloping off
along the plateau. Another appeared from behind a rock and
for a full moment they stared vis-à-vis, whisker to whisker almost, it seemed through the field glasses; then both disappeared
behind the rock at the same moment as yet another came into
view. For a while there seemed to be an unending circle of

hares, and I began to wonder whether there were three or thirty. But by the time I had clambered over the boulders and reached that rock, there was nothing to be seen except a maddeningly busy little pipit. Coming down the last slope toward the point, a long, gentle slope of tightly packed gravel and small stones, studded with brilliant patches of saxifrage, I came across what must have been the Eskimo equivalent of FRED THONG WAS HERE 1971 or BRENDA LOVES CHUCK in white paint on a roadside cliff: small round boulders neatly laid out to form syllabic characters. Some of them had been placed there long enough for saxifrage and avens to grow in and around the characters, and some seemed quite recently placed. The whole slope looked like a tidy rock garden. And when a few minutes later I came upon Jobee sitting on a rock I almost laughed out loud: from his pointed hood to his tiny feet in sealskin boots, he looked so exactly like a plaster garden gnome.

But instead of a fishing rod, Jobee was intent with his brass-bound telescope. It was supported on a stick before him, and he had it trained on the far cliffs beyond the river. I sat down beside him, and presently he passed me the telescope. But it was only after a long time and much patient resighting on Jobee's part that I was able to see what he had been watching: a very large bird perched so utterly still on a cliff ledge and merging so easily into the shadows that it was small wonder my inexperienced eye had not picked it out. I was just trying to keep the telescope steady enough to try and identify it when it took off — there was a brief but unmistakable glimpse of long pointed wings as it flapped quite slowly across the cliff face — it was a falcon. Only a peregrine could be as big as that, I decided, and got the Peterson *Field Guide* out of my pocket to show Jobee and ask him what the Eskimo name was — he had already written several in syllabics for me. But he shook his head at the peregrine in the illustration (it was called a duck hawk in this edition), and at all the other falcons, then took the book and thumbed intently through the pages until he came to a page of overhead silhouettes of accipiters, falcons and kites, and with a triumphant smile tapped the gyrfalcon there on the head with the stem of his pipe. He told me the name — I had no pencil — but it was difficult to repeat. However, I managed it recognizably enough for John later, and he told me that Jobee was never wrong — he had an eye like a falcon himself.

I grew to admire Jobee more and more — so quiet and unhurried, so seemingly content at all times, and self-sufficient. If the white man and all his so-called benefits had disappeared from the Arctic that day, Jobee would not have missed them, for he had lost none of the survival skills of his people. Nor had he lost any of the knowledge of their games, for his small, deft fingers could weave one version of a string game after another, or juggle unerringly with stones. He could have been the model for a thousand Eskimo carvings — little round men bending from the hips over seal holes, little round men crawling along with harpoons in their hands, little round sorcerer men with two heads, etc., etc. Susan said that after a week in his company her sketchbook would be filled with little round men bending over, and I could quite understand why, for I could hardly keep my hand off the camera button, at first, every time he did anything whatsoever. He spoke no English, and my vocabulary was limited to about fifty words, but somehow we got along, and I found him wonderfully helpful in identifying animal bones and their particular anatomical place. I would produce one of the countless bones with which my pockets always seemed to be stuffed, and he would say netchuk — seal, or tuktuk — caribou, then tap the corresponding bone on his own body. One time when I produced two small bones that I had thought were part of a seal flipper — for I was trying to collect my own components for the bones-in-a-bag game — he laughed and pointed to his own fingers, then himself: they were human bones. He laughed even more when I buried them with embarrassed haste in the turf.

I think perhaps, looking back, that he may have been keeping an eye on my progress down the mountain as well as on the gyrfalcon, for I must have been away far longer than I realized — everyone had eaten whatever meal it was we were supposed to have eaten and had retired to their tents, all except Eberhard who had gone out with the hunters — and the two dog teams I had watched heading out from my eyrie were just coming in under the rocks now. At any rate, he replaced his beautiful, old telescope in its case now and walked back with me. But perhaps he was just going to meet the teams — one could never tell.

I heated up the remains of the stew and took my share down to the rocks to watch. With the komatiks lurching across the water pools and hummocks, the dogs covered the last quarter of a mile at a gallop, and came straight up the narrow gulley below me, jumping up on the rocks as the komatik slid to a halt. There, still in fair shape, they lay down immediately to lick their unbooted paws and as much of the others as possible (they never attempt to take the boots off). There were two quite large seals on Joatanee's komatik. The three small figures of the Eskimos, their fur-trimmed parka hoods up against the wind, moved along the teams, sorting things out in some complicated pattern: one dog unhitched and dragged to another place — Jobee so small that he barely had to bend to unhitch, and would not have looked too out of proportion astride; another given a good kick for trying to pick a fight, or for lying possibly in the wrong place (or just to remind him not to pick a fight or lie in the wrong place; I could never tell the unobvious Goodies from the Baddies). Two or three were let loose and immediately set off for a boat on the ice, where, standing on their hind legs, they delved down, two of them bringing up some unidentifiable delicacy which they tore at, holding it down on the ice with a paw — the third, either too lazy or late, jumped the first and a brisk and noisy fight ensued, terminated by a well-directed chunk of ice from Oodlateetah. In the meantime, dog two had gulped his own piece, then quietly filched the one in dispute, and was now beating a strategic retreat to the rocks. The big black dog we called the Shop Steward was causing trouble as usual, his face thrust close to his long-suffering teammate, his lips drawn back, he rumbled threats and taunts, spoiling for a good set-to: a rock landed on his aggressive, bushy hindquarters and he subsided, muttering into his whiskers for a while. One small bitch, whom I had never seen punished, even when she had been trotting along with her trace sagging, pushed against Jobee's knee, wagging her tail, curving her hindquarters in affection — the only tail wagging in the company — but her overtures went unrecognized. The men looked at paws, the dogs lying back with that ears-laid-back, poor me, hypochondriacal look common to all dogs as the sealskin boots were removed. With only a few surly comments from the Shop Steward, the dogs settled down, and the men departed for the hut and stew. They had seen three narwhals and a walrus at the floe edge, and had shot the seals on the way back. So the dogs would have a good feed later. I saw our lame follower from Bylot, staked now, but no sign of the dog we had left on the ice. Joatanee said a hunting party they had met had not seen it on the way out, so it may well have recovered and returned to Pond.

I encountered the other members of our party from time to time, crowded into the hut for meals produced by John. The subsequent washing-up was usually performed by Susan and me — in a small plastic bowl that doubled for ablutions as well — assisted very often by Eberhard, in return for which we poured him into his darkroom, which he kept with his sleeping bag on the sleeping platform, safe from plate-scraping desecration. This was quite an operation, involving Eberhard stripping down to his vest, shuffling along the platform, semibagged, then entering the bin like a homing whelk. Muffled instructions would issue from inside, then silence, while we wondered whether he had suffocated, and finally a backward emergence, dripping, with triumphant beet-red face and sweat-stained blond beard.

Sometimes the temperature was reasonable; sometimes it was so cold that drinking water froze solidly in the tent, and the only way to get warm enough to write or read was to fill an empty lime juice bottle with hot water and huddle into one's sleeping bag. For reading material I had a book on Arctic exploration — material that had been gripping enough to me all my life, but here had a special significance, for this part of the Arctic occurred time and time again in the accounts of attempts to discover the Northwest Passage. (Even before that, for Erik the Red discovered Baffin Island, and it seems likely from one of the few existing records that a party of Norsemen from the Greenland settlement landed on Bylot.) Bylot Island had been named more than three centuries ago after Robert Bylot, the incomparable navigator who had brought the *Discovery* back to England following the casting adrift of its captain, Henry Hudson, by the mutineers. He returned again and again with William Baffin to these seas in the search for the passage, as did Thomas Button, whose namesake we were camped on now.

Baffin and Bylot made the first circumnavigation of the bay on whose frozen surface we had camped. That was in 1616.

We came into an open sea on the latitude of 75 degrees 40′, which revived our hopes of finding a passage (to the north). Because the wind was contrary we stood twenty leagues from the shore before we met the ice, then standing in again, when we were near the land, we let fall an anchor to see what tide there was, but we found small comfort in that.

The date was July 1 — and so was the date on my journal, on the day I read that — so three and a half centuries ago I could have looked out of my tent that very day and seen the gallant little *Discovery* off the floe edge.

It would have been superfluous to write of the weather because it was so variable; there were few days without snow and it was often freezing, our ropes, shrouds and sails so frozen that we could scarcely handle them; yet the cold is not so extreme that it cannot be endured.

He would not have found conditions very different today, I thought, turning the pages with purple-mittened fingers, and equally variable, for one day I wakened to the patter of raindrops and the turf floor turned to a soggy bog. The hut was as sordidly uninviting too: every seam of the plywood roof running, bowls, tins and pots everywhere to catch the drips, and a steady plink, plonk, pong which I duly recorded for my symphony. Only the immediate space by the walls was dry; we covered everything in garbage bags, wrung Eberhard out, and departed for the varying comforts of our tents. We found small comfort in ours. I would have given a great deal to move in with the Eskimos at that point; they had a Coleman stove in their tent, and looked very snug.

But sometime in the night the wind changed and the mist cleared. I woke to the sun baking the tent wall at my head, and the sound of snow geese very close — so close, in fact, and so low, that the enormous shadow of their wings passed over the tent. They were heading for the river so I decided to follow them there.

The river lay to the east, glacially fed, rushing now through the long valley to the bay, forced to straighten and cut deeply in its last half mile by the steeply flanking mountains. Many years ago there had been a semipermanent settlement on its high grassy banks, and even a white trader; but the evidence of habitation went far back beyond those days to Thule and Dorset times, and perhaps even beyond.

It was a wet walk, and a long one, for I was in a hurry to get there before the geese left, and tried to follow the coast — only to find that the long gullies were filled with deep snow, and the whole plateau was a deceptive waterfield beneath the bright new grasses from the runoff on the hills. I leaped from tussock to tussock, and when I missed my boots often sank glutinously over their tops into patches of melting clay below the water. After extricating one foot out of its boot and then the other for about the fifth blasphemous time, I looked up to see the geese passing directly overhead — heading out toward the bay again.

I suddenly thought how silly I must seem to them, bringing my white heritage of hustle-bustle to a timeless land, getting cross and seeing nothing in my hurry to get somewhere and see something that wasn't going to be there when I arrived. . . . So I took my boots off and squished slowly and pleasantly through the oozy clay until I came out on a dry gravelly ridge, and there I sat for some restoring eons of time.

There was a pool below me, reflecting white cumulus and a ring of low Arctic willow, the buds tinged with carmine, as softly haired as the inside of a dog's ear; and stretching from there a yellow carpet of the little Arctic buttercups, a soporific bee droning industriously over it. The high-pitched piping of ivory gulls feeding on something on the ice was borne in on the wind, while closer to hand a raven quoth very loudly and received a croaking echo comment in return from the cliff. Far, far away the banks of cumulus lay so low over the mountains that it looked almost as though they were spilling their whiteness down the sweeping highways of the glaciers, then flowing out over the ice to drown at last in reflection.

Seals were basking by their holes. I basked too, warm and

content and ambitionless — other than to improve my aim with a handful of raisins at the inevitable Lapland longspur perched stolidly on a rock a few yards away.

I found the Thule house remains eventually on the slope near the river mouth, the same semiunderground circle of boulders with the long narrow porches as at Pond and Quilalukan. Some distance away were the foundation outlines of what must have been the trader's house: two circles, much larger than those of the Thule houses, the walls formed of boulders that still retained some considerable height, and the remains of wooden uprights marking the passageway. One site was probably the store, the other living quarters. A curved caribou bone with a hole drilled through lay half-buried by one entrance, part of a roof tie, I learned later from Jobee. A whole vertebra stood in the middle of the other site, with a row of nails hammered in on one flange, for no reason that I — or even Jobee, later — could think of, unless it was some strange new musical instrument the trader was in the middle of inventing. Bright patches of yellow avens were growing now where his floor must have been. Sitting on the enigmatic vertebra, listening to the river sounds, I tried to imagine what it must have been like to have lived here. If he had been Scottish (and most traders were), he would not have found the landscape behind very different from his homeland: the long valley into the hills beyond, the river winding through, carving and polishing its snowbanks to ice, could be any Highland glen in winter. Sitting today among the outline of caved-in, overgrown walls, I could have been in one of a hundred ruined sheilings in Argyllshire.

Crossing the plateau farther up on the way back I came on some graves: mounds of boulders, with sometimes smaller circles of boulders at the foot. Part of a skull lay on top of one, and bones were scattered here and there — the lengths of tibia and fibula being immediately recognizable. Farther on, near a marshy part with no visible grave nearby, lay the rounded plate of a human cranium. Thinking it must belong to the skull, I took it back to reunite them, only to find that it didn't match. Strange that here I had none of my usual feelings on beholding a human skull — that this amazing grinning object was once a thinking, seeing being like me, and that (unbelievably) I shall look like that one day — for this land is so filled with bones, packed in the short space of earth above the permafrost, or bleaching on the turf and shores, that these human remnants held no more significance than just another bone or two.

Before the coming of the missionaries there was no Eskimo burial — not that complete burial would have been possible with the permafrost, but even a shallow grave with piled-up boulders was not used — the body was left in a sealed-up igloo, tent or dwelling, and that was that. Later foxes or wolves would break in and the bones would be scattered, along with any possessions, so it is very rare that an ancient skeleton is found; in all his years of Arctic exploration Father Mary had only once found a pre-Dorset skull. And as there were no graves, so there could be no informative grave furnishings for future archaeologists to uncover. There can be no Arctic Sutton Hoo, or Tutankhamen's Tomb.

Almost all accounts of Eskimos, from earliest times to the present century, contain references to the total lack of dismay or apprehension expressed over death, and the disinterest in the hereafter. Successive waves of Christian explorers found this very strange, burdened as they were with the doctrine of original sin and a lifetime struggle to overcome it for fear of the wrath to come. Life itself was enough for the Eskimo people, apparently, as happy and plentiful a life as possible, and to have lived sufficient reward; misery was an unknown word, an unconceived state, so that miserable sinners were as far removed from reality as the concept of a white race.

The Christian message must have been very confusing for the
Eskimos. Why worry about death when whatever happens after
it can only be reckoned in terms of benevolence? If they were
lucky enough they might go down below, to a pleasant region
presided over by Imammeengunga, the Lady of the Sea. The
next best was upstairs with her brother, Aningak. After that,
rather dull and prosaic, but nothing dreadful about it, was the
middle, looked after by Socrinak, the spirit of the sun. (When I
heard about these beliefs, from a Swedish anthropologist at
Pond, it occurred to me that perhaps the best place, beneath
the sea, would not be the most peaceful, for Imammeengunga
sounded as though she might be rather prone to moods, and
those dependent on the living:

Sometimes when people do foolish things, Imammeengunga gets
cross, and her hair gets dirty then (presumably from throwing herself
around in a tantrum) and filled with sand; and the Angakkoq must
leave his corporal body and travel down to the sea and calm her, and
comb the sand and seaweed out of her hair, so that she will send the
seal and whale and walrus back.

Sometimes I wondered what Joatanee and Jobee thought as
they worked on the site, and the bones of the meals their forefathers ate were uncovered, along with their toys, weapons and
objects of beliefs and superstitions whose meaning has long
since been lost — or not? — from the chain of handed-down
knowledge. Particularly Jobee, who was no anachronism here,
who could still carve the intricate fishing spear points and hooks
from ivory. Father Mary, who is fluent in the proper scholarly
Eskimo of Jobee's generation, may have asked him, or gleaned
some knowledge; but if he has, like all archaeologists trained to
accuracy and the disregard of high-flown premise, with a built-
in fear of misquotation and misrepresentation, he keeps it
strictly to himself.

There was room for only two or three people to work on the official site. John and Father Mary between them finished the initial heavy labor by the end of the first day, and the six feet or so of darkly gleaming cliff face was beginning to look very ship-shape and squared off. After this they were down to the more delicate, probing work, chipping away at the ice around the layers of protruding bones. Joatanee worked a little farther along, while Jobee was more often engaged in his own little dig on the top. Both of them had accompanied Father Mary on his trips before, and knew exactly what to do.

It was possible all round the banks of the peninsula to choose a personal site for excavation, one of the turf-topped columns of peat and humus broken off by erosion and lying toppled on the slope being the best, as they were free of frost and easy to explore. Anything they contained would probably be lost by the following season to the action of snow and ice, so the amateur, however inept, could not harm, and his salvage could only be welcomed. The next stage, still harmless, was sitting on top of the bank and slicing a neat gully down to permafrost level. One took paper bags along to the chosen sites: any chippings or artifacts found were dropped in, and the bag left there, to be numbered and marked off on the area plan in due course; bones were left in a pile to be examined for anything unusual.

I was very lucky my first time. Having selected a site on the unarchaeological principles of (a) it being sheltered from the wind and (b) there being no evidence of blubber or dog where I proposed to sit, I set to work with trowel and fingers: cutting in with the trowel, then crumbling the dry peat so that nothing was lost. As the turf column was almost upside-down one was able to get at the most exciting part first — the oldest layers. In a relatively short time my paper bag contained two harpoon heads, the flat oval base of a whale baleen cup, a piece of seal-skin folded over some perfectly preserved feathers, many flint

chippings, and two microblades — the little serrated cutting
blades — the latter being only about a quarter inch wide and
one and a half inches long, like thin slivers of flint, yet the edges
so finely worked that when I tried one out across the finger of
my leather glove it sliced through easily. There were many
bones too, caribou and seal; and enough of the round one-inch-
diameter vertebrae discs of seals to start a modest button fac-
tory. On my way up the bank I picked up, en passant, a third
harpoon head, and dropped it in my pocket for the time being.

Sometime later I remembered it, wiped off the dirt, and had a
good look at it: it was a very nice harpoon head, in perfect condition; with some lick and my jacket sleeve I rubbed it up to a
satisfying luster. I decided to ask Father if I might keep this one
as a souvenir.

I have an eye that unerringly falls for the most expensively
unobtainable item before it sees the price. It did not fail me
now. Father Mary, who had to be shown something very rare
indeed to wax enthusiastic, positively glowed over my harpoon
head. It was pre-Dorset, as were the other two, but this one was
very unusual, apparently, the internal insertion cut being rectangular (or something like that) instead of something else.
Sadly, I watched it disappear into the bag of specials for dis-
patch to Ottawa. At least I showed good taste.

The peace of Button Point was rudely shattered on the weekend, when the noise of the first skidoos was heard: the hunters
en route to the floe edge, already towing boats, or coming to
pick them up. Kaminah brought Colly, with young Christopher
and a young Eskimo girl, so now there were thirteen of us
crowding into the hut for meals.

At one point there must have been four or five skidoos on
the ice, and a goodly congregation of little dark people all
standing around, warming up with tea, or helping Elijee, who
had just arrived, to get his machine in working order again. It

had gone through the ice, sliding off the komatik and straight
into deep water. Fortunately a rope was trailing and they were
able to haul it out. Watching them eventually disappearing into
the mist, I suddenly longed to see the floe edge again, to recapture
and regenerate some of the magic there that had never
entirely left me all the year. So I woke Oodlateetah and asked if
he would take me out. He was only too delighted to have something
to do, for he seemed to have no interest in working on the
site like the others, and in no time at all had the team hitched
up, and his rifle and teabox aboard. Eberhard, restless for fresh
photographic fields, decided to come too, and the team was only
too delighted at some action. The other dogs lifted their voices
in an envious chorus, and the Shop Steward expressed his
displeasure with a furious onslaught on one of our team who
passed rashly close.

The empty komatik felt strangely low at first, with only a
caribou skin over the slats. The mist was by now so thick that
the point disappeared almost immediately, even though we
were running quite close to the shore, and there was now a
widening crack of open water to be negotiated before we could
get out onto the flat. This we crossed at a nasty-looking gap
temporarily bridged by a floating raft of ice. Eberhard and
Oodlateetah got off, then to shouts and whip cracks of encouragement
the dogs leaped the initial gap, two or three of them
falling in and scrabbling desperately at the ice edges until
hauled up and on by the still-traveling team. I stayed on the
komatik, keeping my eyes averted from the depths and with a
good handhold on the lashings as the long curve of the runners
headed for the gap. But what I was afraid would happen —
that the icepan would capsize with me and the dogs aboard (I
had already picked out the one I was going to hang on to when
we went) — didn't, of course, for Oodlateetah had known his
ice since childhood. As the runners slid easily across and over,

he leaped on behind me at the last moment. Eberhard took a run at it and his long legs hurdled the gap with a foot to spare.

Sometimes, on treacherous ice, or on horrid loose icepans that slewed sluggishly then worked themselves up to a mean rock, we had to perform a crossing operation which involved sending the dogs over first, then cutting the main trace loose, after which the komatik was carried over — in case the dogs started up again too suddenly and the runners, pointing toward the water, were caught on the overhanging edges of ice. I always found this rather an unnerving procedure, hoping that I would not disgrace myself with a slip at the final moment of my leap, and praying to land fair and square on the caribou-skin target. But a good healthy fear certainly does wonders for athletic accuracy. Once, when the dogs were cut loose like this, they set off at a gallop. Oodlateetah must have taken seconds off the hundred-yard-dash record going after them — he managed to get hold of the trailing trace, hauling back with his heels dug in, but the dogs were going so fast that he went skimming over the ice for quite a way, only halted by the team dividing round a hummock.

Sometimes when the dogs leaped a gap and one or two fell in, the komatik went straight over their heads, powerless to stop, and each time there would be heart-rending yowls from the water, so ghastly that I dared not look down, not wanting to see the mangled remains. But somehow the heads always bobbed up again unharmed, and as the komatik slid on, the dogs would either be hauled out backward on the end of their traces as the team went on, or one or other of us would grab the harness in passing and give a helping hand. They seemed very gay and different today, despite all the trauma, probably realizing that this was just a jaunt. We had only taken seven, leaving the lamest to rest, but presently the usual follower appeared to trot alongside. Whenever they spotted a seal ahead, the komatik would take a great leap forward as they broke into a gallop — unchecked by Oodlateetah, for if a young seal has strayed too far from its hole a team can often run it down.

At one point their distant black dot target turned out to be only a crippled murre. This time Oodlateetah halted them, anchored the komatik with a heavy grappling iron, and ran after the bird. He brought it back to photograph cradled in his arms, one wing trailing broken; but, set down on the ice, the bird skittered away into the mist. Later the rush was for a dying eider (sadly, its mate was standing beside it), and the big black second dog caught it up in his mouth. Oodlateetah took it from him, and gave it to me to hold while he disentangled the team. It was pathetically light, practically skin and bones; a beautiful northern bird, with black markings above the bill coming to a V instead of the U of the common eider, and the most beautiful dusting of pale green behind the lusterless eyes. Oodlateetah dispatched it quickly, then dropped it into the teabox to skin later. The mate circled us twice, then disappeared into the mist.

Eberhard and I had made a pact before we left — not to intrude upon the peace and silence of this mist-shrouded ice world with talk. So it was especially quiet out there, and ghostly, everything muffled, and only the sound of the dogs' paws splashing through stretches of water, or the occasional whish of fast-beating wings as unseen flocks of murres passed overhead. Before us the tracks of the skidoos led into a horizonless world. For a while it seemed as though we were traveling in some dream eternity, with no landmarks or even variations in ice formation visible.

Then suddenly, as though a curtain had been lifted in the mist, those incredible gleaming white battlements before the floe edge appeared, and we came through into a dazzling brilliant world of sunshine, alive with sound, heady with the fresh salt smell of moving water. It was like a miracle.

After the silence of the mist the screaming of the fulmars was almost overwhelming, the reflected glare from ice and water too intense for one pair of sunglasses. Everything was almost too much for me altogether: it is so seldom that we return to the places that we have loved best without diminution of some sort.

There was a layer of powdery snow over the ice, soft and easy going for the dogs. They padded jauntily along the white road winding around bays framed in dark blue water or with a slowly moving frieze of ice sculptures, past tuskless narwhal skulls and curving empty rib cages lying like stage props in the wings — a peaceful, surrealistic world — until suddenly we heard coming toward us the horrid effrontery of a skidoo engine, laboring. And no wonder, for it hauled a boat with at least seven Eskimos inside, a broken-down skidoo, several seals and a hefty chunk of narwhal. We halted and talked for a while, when they told us that there was no chance of our reaching the hunters, as they were several miles on beyond a wide crack negotiable only by boat. So we stayed where we were to photograph, by a small channel of blue open water.

Eberhard photographed with all the perfectionist care of a professional: bending over a reflection for seemingly hours, waiting for the right moment, changing lens after lens, camera after camera. Then came the action shots: getting Oodlateetah to drive the puzzled team first in one direction, then turn and wheel in another, so that he could press the button at the exact dramatic moment. He wanted a passenger, so, trying to look as relaxed and like an Eskimo as possible, I stayed on board the komatik and was whirled around too. At one point I was laughing so much (at the spectacle of Eberhard running like mad ahead of us so that he could take up station to record the onrushing team, shouting instructions over his shoulder as he fled) that I fell off at the buildup of the final swerve. By this time both Oodlateetah and I were almost hysterical, and even the dogs were either getting their "oys" and "aie-ee's" mixed or beginning to clown, too, for the traces looked like a cat's cradle. So Eberhard gave up, and photographed the primitive skills of Oodlateetah making tea on the stove instead.

The run back was beautiful beyond belief, shadows long on the sunlit ice, the mountaintops emerging above the mist beyond. The four little tents perched on the end of Button Point looked like a welcoming village from miles away.

It was past midnight when we climbed the bank, and I thought everyone would have been fed long ago, but we found them just about to eat; no one had any idea of the time, for there had been much excitement: half a mask had been found. As Father Mary recounted, he had just removed a stone, and was standing there, looking down, resting a moment, when "suddenly there was a little 'pouf,'" and out dropped the mask at his feet. It was the same reddy-brown color, with the same type of little pegs, but rounder-cheeked than the other; the nose was missing, and two small slivers from the forehead (apparently these masks were made from three pieces of wood, glued together, with, possibly, a form of glue made from fish roe). The place from where it dropped out was almost directly behind where the first mask was picked up, so perhaps this really was a sorcerer's "grave."

Now, like the prospect of an exciting dip into a bran pie, was the thought of the other half waiting its turn to be released from the permafrost.

It would have to wait for twenty-four hours, for tomorrow was Sunday, when no work would be done on the site, and when the rest of the party was to start back to Pond. I was to inherit John's snug, windproof tent. Selfishly, I could hardly wait for them to go, so that I could move in and a working Monday roll round the faster.

❧ Chapter 8 ❧

It was strange not to see any heads rimming the edge of the point, or hear the sounds of shovel and trowel. Even the dogs were quiet. As in an Eskimo village, no one stirred until about noon, when they heard Father Mary beating an oil drum with a caribou bone and shouting "First call to breakfast."

Later he celebrated mass in his tent, with a congregation of two, Susan and Katerina. On his field trips he always takes along what he calls his portable chapel, a box with all the necessities of the mass, including a cassock and even candles for the altar, which in this case was an up-ended food box in the inner tent. Later, carrying a compass, he walked around the plateau with measured tread, leaving a trail of white markers behind him. Then with furrowed brow he retired to his tent to work out his calculations — mathematics were not his strong point, he said sadly — and write up his notes.

By late afternoon the others had folded their tents and were about to steal away in the loaded komatiks. As though she were dividing the remaining supplies like Franklin and Hood, Susan left me with some Arctic essentials and comforts, carefully dividing the chocolate and Mother McCree's Best Cough Syrup for

the return ordeal: heroically she even divided her personal supply of peppermints. I was as moved by this as by that altruistic
early voyageur, Perrault, who saved his own ration of pemmican
to hand around as a nice surprise for his companions when
they had just finished the last of their shoe leather. I felt this
even more when I watched the party take off in the two teams
and saw that there were four and a half people perched on her
komatik. Moreover, she had a very bad cold: she would need
every peppermint she could get, even Mother McCree herself,
to get her through the next fifteen hours of cold, cramped
traveling.

I filmed their departure, the teams winding in and out of
crack leads. By ones and twos the hunters came and went, until
the last engine throbbed out of range. Then silence and peace
came dropping slow on Button Point and I retired to my luxu-
rious, double-walled tent.

After twenty-four hours' abstinence, Father Mary was probably down on the site at one minute after midnight on Monday.
He was certainly there before breakfast, when I went down, and
very excited: he had just uncovered the two missing fragments
off the side of the mask — one sliver still had three little pegs
sticking out of it. We took them up to his tent, and fitted them
onto the half mask most satisfactorily. Not very long afterward,
back on the site, I picked out a loose piece of wood on the end
of the trowel, saw that it was shaped, and handed it to Father
for identification — and even in midair he recognized it: "It's
the *nose!*" he said. And sure enough it was, fitting smoothly and
perfectly into place, as though it had never been parted for all
those centuries.

Now, with a few more little stones removed, and some more
careful picking away at the ice by Father, we saw peeping out
of its frosty prison what looked like the outside rim of the sec-

ond half of our mask. Most tantalizing, for nothing could be
hurried now; the frost must set the piece free naturally if it were
not to be damaged.

Joatanee had joined us, and we turned from temptation and
worked at other faces of the site. He, like Jobee, had often been
on digs with Father, and worked steadily, puffing away on his
pipe, seemingly absorbed. He was a good-looking young man,
about twenty-five, with a wide, most delightful smile, the son of
an old friend and traveling companion of Father's, Annakudlip,
and of Annavapiak who had died last year. From time to time,
when a dog whined, he would turn and scan the ice beyond.
Suddenly, after a particularly insistent whine, he was gone, and
the next moment his team was heading out. Shortly after, we
heard the crack of a rifle shot; the team came galloping back
with a seal trailing on a rope behind the komatik. Five minutes
later Joatanee was back beside us, still puffing on the same pipe.

Sometimes I picked away around a protruding bone with the
trowel point, or scraped with the edge; sometimes I could gently
peel down a mat of loosened peat off the smooth frost, then
search among it with my fingers as it hung there. Occasionally I
found a flint chipping, and very occasionally, at the level I was
working on at present, a microblade or a point. Beside the
usual paper bag we now had the Doug Bag and the Ash Bag:
the former being for birdbone identification by Doug Heyland,
the latter for a Mr. Ash who wanted specimens of any wood
found. (He was an energetic American octogenarian who had
arrived out of the blue at Pond in his own plane last year, and
spent several days there, becoming so interested in Father's archaeological project that he left his 8mm movie camera so that
some film of this dig could be made for him.)

A wooden stick carving of a seal was gradually uncovered,
then a human figure — both about three inches long and one
inch thick. The latter had a crudely sketched face, the knob of

head tapering into the rectangular "body"; across the chest was a cut, the "Dorset slash" which features in all these carvings, and for which there is no known significance, only the possibility that "killing" the image might bring hunting success with the reality. Sometimes effigies of game had the slit between the shoulder blades. Then a bear, with faint red stains, continuing to bear out a conclusion which Father Mary was approaching, that the bear miniatures were this color, while seals were stained black.

Sometimes we talked; most of the time we were contentedly silent. When we talked it was not about archaeology (alas, for I would have loved to learn more), but about things like childhood and school. Chilblains occupied us for quite a time; we remembered them with mutual vivid discomfort, and it occurred to us that no child on this side of the Atlantic ever seems to have them nowadays. "Sometimes they are so bad," reminisced Father unexpectedly in his precise, accented English, "that I must put my hands under my ass and sit on them!"

Looking at his hands now, very white, with long thin fingers and beautifully shaped nails, it was difficult to imagine them red and swollen with itching fingers; it was a pleasure to watch them at work around some protruding artifact, delicately probing, brushing off particles of dirt with a little whiskbrush.

There was a slight contraction of the fingers of the right hand; and it is something of a miracle — or sheer determination — that he has the use of it at all, or that the hand is even there, for medical opinion was that the arm should be amputated after an appalling injury to it some years ago. He was making a film about the Netsilik Eskimos of Pelly Bay, when his skidoo crashed down into a gully, and the following komatik slid on down on top of him: the runners missed his head by inches and crashed into his shoulder instead.

He told me a story that old Koonah had given him about the

nearby cliffs of Akpah, about a man who was treacherously left there among the nesting murres by his wife's father, but survived, living on the eggs, to reappear in due course at his wicked father-in-law's camp and do away with him. Another story was about a murderer with ten to his credit, who, not unnaturally, became so afraid of retaliation from his victims' relatives that he sat always with a sharp knife point at his forehead, the hilt on his knee, so that if he dozed off and his head nodded, the pain would waken him. He used to go aboard the whalers in order to sleep in safety.

Scraping away with my trowel, millimeter by millimeter as the frost melted, I sometimes longed to seize a pickax and hack on blindly, to get down to all that nitty-gritty at the bottom. Sometimes it seemed as though the pre-Dorset culture was entirely gastronomic. It was the layers of bones that I found so maddening: caribou bones could be massive, but even the delicate bones of hare or the little knuckles of seal could obstruct for ages. When the frost crystallized like quartz among sand particles it could mislead one into exciting expectations of microblades or points.

Like any rubbish dump today, this ancient midden had its smell. It was a strange smell, not altogether unpleasant at first, like a mixture of rather high Harris tweed and wood smoke, only stronger. But on warm days it became decidedly stronger, with a cloying essence of decaying compost heap added, and an indefinable something else — a touch of unsatisfactory drains and old potting sheds, perhaps? When it became too overwhelming I would retreat for a while on the pretext of some pressing domestic chore — like taking the tea towels for a walk around the ice, looking for just *exactly* the right crack in which to rinse them. Navigating by the position of the sun in relation to the heat on the site, this crack sometimes took a long time to find. Father seemed to be immune to the smell. Joatanee wreathed his face in a protective barrier of pipe smoke, but I noticed that he visited the dogs more often than usual during warm spells. They would pant thirstily on the rocks in the sun, and he would break off a chunk of ice and throw it to them to lick, but whether from compassion or nausea it was impossible to tell.

Domesticity was not a feature of Button Point. In fact, I found myself slipping further and further back down the centuries; a few more weeks and I would have been indistinguishable from Mrs. pre-Dorset herself: prodding into peat turves on my walks with a bit of handy caribou bone, tightening the camera screws with a bit of flint scraper found in my pocket, even cutting a piece of sealskin rope for the hut door handle with a microblade; wielding — very, very seldom — my goose-wing brush on the hut floor, or dusting off the debris from a fallen biscuit before resuming consumption. I had been relieved at the outset to find that Father shared the same time-saving ideas about washing dishes: *i.e.*, one bowl, one spoon per capita per diem, and if you are squeamish about spooning Jell-O onto the remains of your stew (I alone had this hang-up) then wipe the bowl with a piece of toilet paper, a roll of which hung on the end of the drying pole suspended from the ceiling. It hung there not so much for kitchen convenience as to stop the rod from piercing some white person's eye or mouth as he entered the hut, Eskimos being so short that they would pass under. And to use more than one mug during the day would be sheer dissipation.

Father was able to add another thrifty culinary hint: never clean off the morning's porridge saucepan. That crusty, hard-set ring and those deposits cemented to the bottom will soften up under lunchtime soup and thicken it into the bargain. And the debris of lunchtime soup, naturally, will increase the flavor of supper's stew. I don't know if this premise extends into supper's stew improving next morning's porridge, for even I drew the line there, and faithfully cleaned out the pot at this stage. But really only for my own satisfaction, for after a while, I realized that, while Father's body may have gone through the physical motions of eating, the rest of him was wandering around pre-Dorset times. And I think that if I had boiled up a few period bones, thrown in some caribou hairs and seasoned it with coal dross, he really wouldn't have noticed. Joatanee had a wonderfully prodigious appetite, and was probably the best finisher-upper that anyone could hope for in a kitchen.

Sometimes it was warm enough to bring the saucepan down to the point and eat there in shirtsleeves, basking in the sun. Sometimes the wind blew so bitterly that it pierced through parkas and layers of sweaters; eyes streamed and fingers froze, and to the music of pick and trowel was added the uninterrupted sniffing of the three of us.

By the end of the second day the edge of the second half mask lay with its rim outlined in its bed of permafrost. Father had picked the surrounding ice as far back as it was safely possible, and now, tenderly, dusted off the protruding part with his little whisk before leaving it for the night. He spent a long time walking around the area above the site with a long measuring tape and a plumb line concocted from my anorak cord and a stone; then he manufactured a neat white directional arrow pointing to the mask, and planted a sign directly above the site so that it would appear accurately marked, or, as he said, "at least within two or three kilometers": 12 S 5E was printed conspicuously on it for the cameras.

An hour later, checking things over, he realized that something was wrong with his calculations: it should be north, not south — quite a difference. I left him to work it out and write up the day's finds, and retired to my sleeping bag to write up my own journal. "Tuesday evening," it reads, between 6 and 7 A.M. tomorrow the sun will strike directly on the site, the frost should have melted sufficiently to loosen the mask, and we shall photograph it in situ, then the moment of removal. This last operation, historic moment in Arctic archaeology will be recorded by none other than S. Burnford — that camerawoman so notoriously inclined to snap anything momentous with the lens cap on; aware of these deficiencies she has just now taken the precaution of removing the caps before going to sleep, and substituting socks — these, she feels, cannot possibly fail to remind her. Sausages for supper. Snow flurries outside. Dogs are singing.

I called Father the next morning at 7 A.M., and we went down to the site with a fine collection of cameras. Right according to schedule the piece of mask was loose on the ice, ready to remove, the sun directly striking the site. Father photographed it carefully with his Pentax, and I, unknown to him, photographed Father photographing (but so intent and preoccupied was he that it is doubtful if he would have noticed had twenty flashbulbs been set off under his nose). Then came the moment of removal, and with sock safely off, I said "Action!" and zoomed in with the 16mm Beaulieu on his hand as it slid the piece of wood out. Then, so busy that I didn't have time to see anything except through a lens, I picked up the still camera and clicked off on that, and was dutifully reaching for Mr. Ash's 8mm when I heard Father's astonished-disappointed-excited (I only wish that I had had a third hand for the tape recorder as well to record the full nuance) voice: "It's part of *another* mask . . ." And our dreams of fitting the last piece to make the perfect unique whole that morning vanished.

I tried to console Father by saying that at least he knew now that there was a possibility of ending up with two complete masks instead of one, but I don't think it helped much. He was obviously very disappointed at that moment.

The new half was more like the original of last year: a narrower, longer face with upward-slanting Mongolian eyes; whereas Saturday's find had downward-sloping eye sockets, and was rounder in the cheeks. The difference in the direction of the eye sockets was very pronounced, not unlike the Janus masks of tragedy and comedy. This was the comedy half — if the sorcerer had put it on now he would have looked very amused at our antics. Saturday's features would have looked more appropriate on us as we laid the find back to rerecord its removal for Mr. Ash. Then once again we photographed close-ups of the site and the mask at various angles. Having finished the roll, Father suddenly remembered that he had forgotten to change South to North on the location marker above: the developed films would clearly state that we were on the other side of Bylot Island. "Ah, well," he said philosophically, as we went up to the hut and had two big bowls of porridge each in silence, while Joatanee on the platform beside us continued to sleep, snoring gently, the quilt snuggled up over his head. (Some weeks later Father Mary wrote to say that he had been able to make a flying trip back to the site. The second half of the "sad" mask was excavated, and now, after who knows how many centuries apart, the two halves have been reunited in the Ottawa Museum — complete except for the still-missing nose.)

This afternoon we uncovered the half of a little carved kayak. Then a bear, and what looks like the blade end of a miniature paddle — possibly belonging to the kayak? Also a curved, deeply grooved, band of wood which was unidentifiable. Immediately below the empty mask slot in the face of the site is a large round boulder, firmly embedded in the permafrost, and obstructing the most promising area behind. If only we had a blow torch, or a nice hot fan.

A blow torch might have damaged wood, even if we had had one, and the nearest plug for a nice hot fan was at Pond. But Father, after a thoughtful siesta, emerged from his tent with the brilliant idea of propping up the Coleman cooker on the food box close to the site, then covering it with his ground-sheet, so that the heat would be deflected on the exposed frost. Eventually, after many combinations and permutations, we erected a Heath Robinson affair with the ground sheet staked to the bank, then draped down over a frame of shovel, broken broom handle and a curved piece of rusty iron found on the beach — this to keep the plastic sheet, which had a tendency to melt, off the Coleman.

In a remarkably short time all became gratifyingly cozy and warm within. We decided to give the sorcerer an hour at this heat, then test to see if tender enough for carving. Father departed up the bank, looking very cheerful, to make the regular short-wave contact with Pond, leaving me to keep an eye on things, and giving a professional promise that he would return in time to exorcise the site if he heard any sudden explosions. Presently I heard his voice. "Over," he finished, and then John Scullion's voice, quacking statically, filled the empty land with news of Pond. There was a message for me: there were two letters and be sure and take my cough medicine. So I took some, and sitting there warming my feet along with the site, I toasted the writer, and then the sorcerer himself for good measure.

After an hour the clay is running freely at the base, although there is no appreciable difference in the icy buttress above. But by tomorrow, things should loosen up. Already we can see part of a carved bear showing, and Father was able to pick out a triangularly sliced sliver of wood with a peg in it — obviously broken off the outside rim of a mask cheek. We tried it on both halves, but it fits neither. So now there are parts of *three* masks — the supply seems never-ending. Unfortunately we don't have enough fuel to keep on heating the site. The wind must be veering — can hear the sound of the river very clearly. Supreme effort of dumplings in the stew tonight.

Not only did the wind veer in the night, but it rose strongly and the weather picture changed completely, with frequent snow flurries.

This morning's hopes for a good melting sun on the site have gone, and it is bitterly cold out there. I wear everything available, including the ground sheet wrapped around, but it doesn't make much difference. Just behind yesterday's bear was a fascinating little figure, about 4″ long and about ¾″ thick. A roughly carved, pointed rather like a coconut, head takes up one third of the length, the rest is just like a squared handle with line incisions at the sides. Where the chest would be are two diagonal slashes, the uppermost one having a hole in the middle, into which has been inserted a twin-ended, waisted-in-the-middle, point — about half as long as the figure itself. One thinks immediately of a wax figure with a witchery needle stuck into it. I sketched it, along with the mask halves, and yesterday's mask part — in the latter the whorls in the wood grain are beautifully worked into the roundness of cheek and chin.

There follow some rather sniveling comments on the pain of returning circulation in the fingers, and the zero temperature of the tent — then an obvious backbone stiffener, stemming from bedtime reading

and always I think about their amazing *literary* fortitude and devotion to duty — Baffin, Franklin, Mackenzie, Bylot — the lot; starving, moribund, frozen, lost, abandoned; wherever they were, sitting out howling blizzards under a dog skin, floating off on an ice pan, prostrate in tents with scurvy — firmly, legibly, with flowery and detailed length, they brought *their* Journals up to date.

(So, *there*, slob, I might have added).

But perhaps there was some justification for my harping on about the cold, for even Father Mary and Joatanee found it too much. The boulder behind which we had hoped to find a trove of artifacts, or at least one of the missing mask counterparts, had finally yielded — with the help of innumerable cups of boiling water poured over — but there was nothing to be seen yet in the recess. Unless the weather changed radically it would be impossible to do any further work this season.

So next time I came down to the site I found it deserted, and Father Mary digging instead in a more sheltered test pit, a neat rectangle cut out of the turf; the part that he was working on had edges tidily and symmetrically cut, with layers as precise as a fruit cake sliced with a knife. In 1962 and 1963 he had dug a series of test pits across the peninsula and suggested I go and try Test Pit 3 or C or whatever it was a little farther on.

I found Test Pit 3 (or C) to be a thoroughly unappetizing sight: about the size of a giant's grave, it had filled up over the years with every conceivable form of rubbish from hunters camped on the point: from rusty tins to an old oil lamp, blubber, garbage bags, and other things I preferred not to look at too closely. There was a vast aesthetic difference between grubbing around in a pre-Dorset garbage dump and today's prime specimen, I found. However, I steeled myself, climbed in and settled down on the foam rubber camera pad for insulation, half of me at least protected from the wind. After a while I was no longer conscious of my unattractive surroundings, the immediate horrors being covered by now with a layer of clods and earth from the trowel. About 15 centimeters down there were a lot of chippings, some microblades, and one worked point, and all the excitement of wondering what lay below them. I was utterly content, even sniffing contentedly, cold hands forgotten. There is something totally absorbing about never knowing what the next scraping will reveal, something that has not seen the light of day for hundreds of years, something inexplicable, or so curiously touching that one cannot help imagining oneself in the place of the human being who made this little blade, that awl.

I had seen a photograph of Button Point taken about sixty years ago in winter, taken from almost immediately below

where I was working: an igloo in the background, some twenty
or so smiling little people in caribou skins standing rigidly facing the camera, a seal skin stretched on a frame on the snow
bank. It was not too difficult to imagine them several hundred
years ago, even a thousand, for until this century the manner of
their life here cannot have altered very much.

(This photograph also bore out a theory why there were so
few "modern," i.e., Thule, artifacts found on the point below
5 centimeters: there had been little change in the sea level over
two thousand years, but much erosion of the point, so that the
later Eskimos built their igloos in the snow accumulated on the
rocky point and lower banks in the winter; thus their garbage,
that would have been today's artifacts, was washed away when
the ice broke up in summer.)

I tried to keep my work as tidy and precise as Father's, but
somehow it never looked quite the same: no matter what, the
edges fluted and the level undulated. My nose ran, my eyes
streamed, my face must have been filthy from continual wiping
with the back of a glove. Only a few short months before I had
been crouched like this, but wiping sweat from my brow, looking at a box of crudely fashioned tools recently uncovered in
the Olduvai Gorge in East Africa, the tools of earliest man. It
had been shimmeringly hot down there at noon, about 104
degrees in the shade — if there had been any. It was shivering
cold here, but if a magic carpet had suddenly appeared I would
not have boarded it to change places.

In the unpredictable way of the Arctic, which makes a nonsense out of arrangement, and turns the people who live there
into philosophers — one of the most frequently used words was
ajagnak, spoken with a cheerful smile of acceptance: loosely,
very loosely translated it means "Ah, well, that's the way the
cookie crumbles" — the weather again changed. The wind

dropped and there was some warmth in the sun, but at the same time the ice conditions changed completely, opening up cracks that would very soon become impassable without a boat: if we didn't go now we might well be marooned until the ice shifted again, or possibly be forced off the ice on the way back, and have to wait it out farther down the coast.

So we left, ironically on the warmest and most windless night for a long time. At least it made travel more comfortable for the first few hours, after the hard work of negotiating the alternately built-up and separating icepans near the shore.

"Am writing this on the komatik on our way back," says my journal rather waveringly that night — the self-admonishment about devotion to the pen must have gone home —

so warm and comfortable on one for once that it's unbelievable. We couldn't have a more perfect night to travel. The komatik is stacked so high with boxes, bags and gear, that it's quite difficult to be nimble leaping on and off. Am sitting on a seal, which is true luxury.

Our shadows were very long and very thin, sometimes traveling with us on the snow, sometimes flitting across blue water so that it looked as though we were flying over the mountains mirrored there. We saw strange recognizable shapes in the icebergs and mountaintops passing by, faces and monsters, bear, fox and an upside-down walrus, the back of an elephant disappearing into the ice, a witch, a woolly mammoth. Father Mary occasionally pointed out various places where he had camped over the years, sometimes intentionally, sometimes trapped there because of the ice. There was one of the latter where, returning from a dig at Button Point with Muqtar and his family, they had been forced to spend two days. "It was not easy to find a campsite," said Father in his mild way; and looking at the massive cliffs of rocky gneiss rising sheer out of the ice I could

see that it was the understatement of the year — it would have
been difficult enough to build a very small nest there.

As usual we had our limping follower, this time a big white
husky who padded along on three paws, dropping farther and
farther behind the young apprentice bitch who ran loose. Sometimes a trace got caught on a sharp overhang of ice; then, if it
was not freed in time, the yowling anchored dog would be
stretched, with the team going on, until the trace snapped.
When this happened they were usually not hitched up again
until the next stop; but instead of enjoying a respite, and having
a look round in their own good time, they invariably returned to
their place among the team, and behaved exactly as though
they were still attached.

There was one exception for a while — a big young extrovert
with a broken trace dangling who was gamboling around like a
puppy, playing catch-me-if-you-can with the team, running
ahead and crouching down to spring as it passed. The team
was very tolerant of all these goings-on, and no irritable elder-
and-better teeth were sunk in his frivolous hide.

As the hours stretched out and it became colder the going
became very hard on the dogs' paws, alternating between long
stretches of water and ice covered by a thin sharp crust of
snow, through which the paws sunk, so that they were cut, not
only on the pads but sometimes on the hocks as well. A few
dogs were booted on all feet, some with one or two; only the
unusually narrow paws of the seemingly indomitable leader,
and the large, thickly furred ones of her second-in-command
went unshod until near the end.

Usually I could turn my mind off about the condition of the
dogs, as I had learned to do many years before when first con-
fronted with the starving, ownerless packs around some Indian
settlements. One had to, or else spend the journey in a useless,
emotional welter. But — tired, possibly, and therefore more vul-

nerable — my eyes following a trail of fresh red prints in the snow, watching a dog dragged along howling as it attempted to defecate, bowled over so that the trace strangled its waist to a hand span, I was no longer able to rationalize or detach my mind. To make it worse, we were reduced to eight dogs toward the last few hours, two having been cut free as they were no longer of any use. More and more Joatanee chirruped encouragingly, but equally more and more the tip of the lash cut home, sometimes three or four dogs at once receiving individual treatment. Only the leader seemed to be spared, and a round, plump perky little bitch who pulled on the shortest and least exacting trace. For hours I had watched her full, furry-trousered hind legs and gay curled tail, trotting jauntily along; but now her tail was flagging, and she could barely pull one booted foot after another, the trace sagging uselessly.

Perhaps she was young, perhaps Joatanee recognized that she had given her utmost, for she had pulled continually well, perhaps she was in whelp — I could not make out the reason for his tolerance, for the most seemingly pathetic dog to me on the outside of the near fan was lashed unmercifully. Eventually, she turned completely around to try and disentangle the trace, and somehow the harness slipped off over her head. She stood there for a long time as the team drew away, her head drooping nearly to the ice; then slowly, and looking very groggy, she followed. By the time we came to the bad ice conditions of Kuktiyuk, and had to stop often to plot and test the route over the icepans, only the constant use of the whip could get the team to its feet again; and even that could not galvanize them into anything more than crawling along at a snail's pace.

Yet this was a good team, and Joatanee one of the best drivers, who valued his dogs. Last year their combined endurance and skill was written into the pages of Canadian Centennial history, when Joatanee was chosen to reenact a record journey under-

taken by Canon Jack Turner, a missionary famous in the Arctic
archives, from Pond Inlet to Igloolik and Moffat Bay, and back
— eleven hundred miles. It was Joatanee's father, Annakudlip,
who had accompanied Jack Turner on the original journey.

For the last two or three hours there was little or no conversation. Father's eyes half closed sometimes, his head drooping,
relaxed as I could never be, for I knew that if I slipped off for a
moment I would almost certainly slip off the komatik too and
be decanted into one of those cold, blue, bottomless seams of
water. I kept myself awake by going through my pockets one by
one (there were at least twenty of them in the layers); and sorting out my pack, holding something between my teeth, securing
something else under a lashing, or gripped between my knees,
then very carefully stowing it all back in again. Living on a
komatik for fourteen or fifteen hours can only be compared for
limitations of space with sailing around the Horn in a dinghy.
And so time passed, until at last we came to a complete halt at
the edge of a 50-yard stretch of open water before the settlement. It was 6:30 A.M. Children, not yet gone to bed, were playing on the shore, small boys were sculling boats, dogs howling
a greeting that was not returned by the exhausted team.

Suddenly John and Colly appeared on the shore, and shoved
off in their big plywood boat. "Good morning," called Colly as
John sculled over, both looking incredibly bright-eyed and
bushy-tailed at this unearthly hour. "Good morning," replied
Father and I, rather more dimly and bedraggled. My legs felt as
though they were made of rubber as we unloaded the dinghy
on the warm sand, helped by a dozen or more children. Taking
only the camera, which had seemingly quadrupled its weight, I
told my rubber legs to climb the hill to the kindergarten.

The last thing I saw, looking out over the ice from my window
before I fell asleep that morning, was the slow centipede of
dragging feet that had been our dog team, crawling back

around the point, and Joatanee's whip arm moving back and forth from the komatik behind. They still had a mile to go before they would be staked out. But at least I knew they would be fed, for I could see the hump of that comfortable seal.

I slept the clock round. And when I eventually went to visit the team they were still sleeping, blinking hazily awake when I approached, expressionless as ever. The dog abandoned on the ice two weeks before was not miraculously restored among them, but the little bitch was joined to the stake chain again, curled up with her nose deep in her thick tail. And loose nearby, foraging the rocks, was the lame follower. A neighboring team set off shortly afterward — one and all, my friends sat up and registered their howling protest at being left behind.

❧ *Chapter 9* ❧

There was a crack as wide as a highway leading from the shore to the Pond Inlet iceberg, and nearly a quarter of a mile of open water below the window. Hundreds of fulmars were moving down the bay with the half-submerged ice, clustered in close curved-wing groups, filling the air with thin shrill sounds as though they were engaged in some ritual. On a firm icepan were some twenty parasitic jaegers, the only large flock that I had seen. Even as I watched, the wind whipped up and veered to drive away the low-lying clouds; like magic the day turned to sharp-cut blue and white, the highway closed as the ice began to move, faster and faster, edging in and cruising past the shoreline, squeaking and groaning, only to open out briefly farther on. Looking down it was as though the whole landscape were moving, the jaegers and gulls adding to the vertiginous effect as they circled and wheeled above it. Flocks of murres flew on a more reassuringly straight course above the whitecaps on the dark open water beyond the restless ice.

On days like this the doors and windows rattled and banged to the wind, and every time someone came in, which was almost all the time, my papers and wild flower collections blew all over the place. It was too cold to walk and nobody was outside — a

wonderful excuse to retire to my cot with the field glasses and
watch the local dramas going on below with the moving ice:

A lone dog out there on a small heaving island of ice — trying to bring
himself to jump for it and swim, then finding himself in such an
intricate pattern of ice floe shapes that it must have been like trying
to find the way out of a maze. I, from this height, could see the key
that would lead to jumping distance of the shore, but he at eye level
had to try each shape in turn, run its length, looking for a jumpable
crack, whining, sometimes pausing to have a good howl. It must have
taken him nearly two hours before he finally made it and came scurry-
ing up the bank below in search of his team mates.

Then there was the everyday saga of the hapless dog team
sailing up and down on their ice raft that daily grew smaller,
the water practically lapping at their paws, the komatik and
skidoo looking as though they were just about to slide off. On
the last possible day, when the pan nudged a mass of ice and
came to a halt about three miles away, a boat put out and I
watched the closing scene through the glasses. The skidoo was
lifted aboard, the komatik then lashed across the gunwales, so
that it looked like a pair of wings, then in jumped the dogs; and
with all their heads pointing the same way, and about two
inches of freeboard, the boat returned. The oil drum must have
been empty for it was left — and nearly drove me mad in the
next week — as it continually sailed up and down before the
window, and every time I caught a passing glimpse of it out of
the corner of my eye I would think it was at least a whale and
rush for the binoculars.

I was very glad to see this particular team returned, to be
staked out on the grass above the rocky embankment just
below, for it contained Marmalade, my baritone lead. Shortly
afterward I was able to record him against the most wonderful
background sounds on the ice, red-throated loons, about eight

of them. Their high, haunting crying started with a rhythmic beat and merged into another part where they sounded as though they were *almost* going to continue into the lovely call of the common loon, but ended there tantalizingly instead.

My baritone was very large, one of the biggest dogs around, with marmalade-fringed ears, and two large round spots immediately above his eyes, which made him look as though he had four eyes. He sang like a virtuoso, with his whole soul, his lower jaw trembling on a particularly long, drawn-out musical howl. His teammates, all sitting with their eyes on him as though he were the conductor, waited until he finished, then one by one took up the chorus. Ootovah, small Levi's mother, who was always climbing up and down the bank to get seal meat from the hut below the team, probably thought I was dotty:

Three times she has come upon me with the tape recorder; once to our mutual embarrassment, when I was trying to get the choir to perform for me by emitting a few little encouraging howls myself, and another time when I had the microphone almost in Marmalade's mouth while he was in full voice; and the third time I was playing the tape back to the pleased, astonished team. She arrives upon the scene so silently in her soft kamiks that I haven't the time to pretend to be picking sorrel or something equally normal before she is upon me. She giggles like mad — then fairly sprints up the hill, either in terror or to regale our neighbors with the next episode. If she should believe, as the Utkuhiksalingmuit do, that the white people are genetically descended from dogs, then here obviously is the living proof.

Sometimes I saw a boat broken loose, and in danger of being cracked like a nut between the opening and closing leads, pursued by its owner jumping from pan to pan. Sometimes when the wind shifted the ice right across the sound to Bylot, leaving clear water by the shore, one or two women would appear, armed with a telescope or a rusty old gun, hoping for a chance pot at the first narwhal to thread its way through the opening leads from the ever-nearing floe edge. And soon after the return from Button Point old Jobee provided me with nearly two days' interest. He was to take his team down to Father Mary's next site on Navy Board Inlet, about eighty miles away. Father Mary and a young assistant from Montreal would get a lift there next time the Otter flew in. I watched the little figure of Jobee load a boat onto the komatik, his pipe stuck in his mouth, looking almost smaller if possible, then pack the boat with all the gear and provisions. He had only gone a short way before he ran into trouble with cracks. One moment I could see the bow of the boat pointing up, the dogs straining their hearts out to get the komatik over the crack — then the next moment it turned over. Two or three Eskimos who had been helping load ran out to help, hurdling the cracks in fine style, and eventually he started off again. But it was a long slow process; not until the following day did the crawling black dot disappear from my view. It was nearly a week later before we were to hear via Father Mary's short-wave scheduled broadcast from the site that the old man had arrived — by boat; he had had to leave the komatik and dogs on Bylot. Dear Jobee, it was to be his last expedition with Father Mary: only a few months later he was in the hospital in Frobisher, where he died of cancer of the liver. I was privileged indeed to have known him.

There would be days when the bay was entirely open water, and the iceberg procession would join in the train of imminent disasters:

Beautiful towering icebergs sailing down from Eclipse Sound. They always seem to be heading straight for ours, so close that I'm almost jumping up and down with excitement, waiting for the crash, and the roar as the vanquished goes over, but somehow they seem to slither by, leaving me like the poor lion that didn't get its Christian. The Imminent Disasters that kept me on my toes all morning were (1)

Super Dumpling on a collision course with the Bastille and (2) two
youngsters after a drifting boat.

Later. The Bastille gave way, and the boys made it to the shore
with half an oar and a piece of floorboard. Creeping quietly over the
willowherb and through the poppy clusters between the rocks, head
and tail low, whiskers bristling in anticipation, goes a striped cat —
progeny of the two imported last year, in search of a lemming for
breakfast.

There was never a dull moment.

About this time, life at the kindergarten received an unexpected bonus in the shape of young Hugh Brody, who came
and went at all hours, using the place as a bolt hole from the
constrictions of the small Eskimo house where he was living
with Inuk and Innuya. The meals could be anytime there, sometimes nothing but bread in the house to nibble on, sometimes a
surfeit of fish; the meat, seal or caribou, was often served raw,
and Hugh's European stomach, while politely partaking, found
it difficult to be satisfied on this diet. Then, when he could get
away, he would come round and fill up at the kindergarten,
working on his notes there at a table in the back room. (Innuya
used to worry about the smallness of his appetite sometimes,
saying that he would starve, little knowing that her adopted son
had already devoured a very adequate helping of baked char,
or good old stew as Mother-used-to-make-it, chez nous.)

Hugh was about twenty-six, a most interesting young Eng-
lishman, who two years before had lived among the dregs of
Indian society in a Canadian city, later publishing a report on
his findings, *The Indian on Skid Row.** In order to be accepted
on Skid Row, where alcohol is a way of life to many, he had
had to learn to down his rotgut with the best, and, as he said,
nearly became an alcoholic himself in the process. As a result of

---

* Hugh Brody, *The Indian on Skid Row* (Queen's Printer, Department
of Indian and Northern Development).

this experience and his report he was asked to return to Canada and do the same sort of in-depth study anywhere he liked. He chose the Eskimos this time, starting with Pond. He had attended the six-week total immersion course in the language at Rankine Inlet, learning enough there to be colloqially fluent, but now he was studying the formal, correct Eskimo, such as Father Mary, alone among the white people at Pond, could speak. His teacher was Annaviapik, a dear old man, very gentle and scholarly, for whom he had the greatest respect and affection; and it was obvious, when he brought Annaviapik round for a formal visit, that the old man had a sincere affection for his pupil. He found it a wonderful language, most logically satisfying, with infinite possibilities of syntax and construction. Words and pronunciation, however, vary greatly from area to area. I was using *Salliq*, an Eskimo grammar compiled mainly from the Coral Harbor area, and would often find after carefully memorizing a phrase or word that it was incomprehensible in Pond.

Hugh was integrating himself in every possible way, going out with the "weekend" hunters as well as on a really tough ten-day fishing trip by dog sled with Innoga, when they netted and cleaned some three hundred fish. He spent almost all the time with his "family" and their friends. Having been accepted into the fold, and with the people's knowledge and approval following a lengthy outlining and discussion meeting, he was now embarked on a project of interviewing the families at Pond, and listening to their ideas of how life should be managed, what was currently wrong, and their opinions of white administration in general. Elizee was accompanying him as interpreter should Hugh's own vocabulary be inadequate.

Because of Hugh's far deeper and more intimate involvement with the people, I was able to learn a lot more about attitudes and beliefs than could ever have come my way from the usual purely social meetings with them, plus the barrier of limited vocabularies on both sides. This meant, that second year, that I did not have to rely on what I was told by white residents, or sensed myself, but could ask Hugh what the people themselves thought.

This coincided with a book I read at the same time, which drew away a great many veils from understanding (and which I wish now had been available many years ago when I first came in contact with the Northern Ojibwa and Cree Indians). It was a book — a printed thesis really — entitled *Eskimo Emotional Expression*,* a title which completely put me off at first, knowing that Jean Briggs was an anthropologist, and expecting therefore the usual twenty-two motive-meanderings and deeply dug interpretations of the common smile, frown or grimace as observed on the faces of some hapless band by a humorless rationalist. Instead of that, it turned out to be the most readable, sensitive, and profoundly helpful work, whether one read it from the language point of view, for which it was intended, or just to gain a better understanding of the people's way of thinking. More than that, it could have a salutary effect on one's relationships with anybody — not just Eskimos — oneself included.

Jean Briggs spent about seventeen months among the Utkuhiksalingmuit people, living *en famille*, learning the language. As she gradually learned the nuances of the language, more and more subtleties of interpretive behavior emerged.

This is from the introduction:

We do often not know exactly what it is in the behaviour of another person that tells us how he is feeling, nor do we know exactly what we have done that makes others recognise how we feel. Even when

---

* Jean Briggs, "Utkuhiksalingmuit: Eskimo Emotional Expression" (Ph.D. thesis, Harvard University, 1967).

we are aware of the behavioural cues which we emit and to which we react, we may be unaware that the same bit of behaviour may have different meanings attached to it by members of different cultures. For both of these reasons — the subtlety of the cues and differences in the meanings attached to them — cultural communication often fails on the emotional level.

Sometimes one hears something, or reads a statement that leaps out at one, like a searchlight, making suddenly and brilliantly clear vague half-formulated ideas at the bottom of one's mind that perhaps one did not even know were there. Then one thinks, "But I always *knew* that, by instinct, or upbringing, or experience or somehow — it is obvious, not new, just written down." And so it is; one *did* know, but the difference is that one did not formulate or apply the knowledge, only stored it away subconsciously. Sometimes it stays stored away forever; sometimes one is lucky enough to come across it as I did this day, competently processed by another more disciplined mind. (It is something like the proverbs: we all know from experience that a lot of people all trying to do the same thing results in confusion, but somewhere, sometime, someone voiced our instinctive knowledge and said simply, "Too many cooks spoil the broth.")

So when I finished this introduction, many things became clear, misunderstandings were set straight, and pitfalls were clearly labeled "Beware." Some I did not know even existed until I had read Jean Briggs. She made no bones about being a perfectly ordinary Kabloonah, albeit an anthropologist, subject to everyday frustrations or irritations, involuntarily relieving them in the normal reaction of a frown or expletive, completely unaware at first of the disapproval with which her family group regarded such natural expressions of emotion. Similarly, when returning a jocular or teasing remark she translated her idiom and facial expression from the customary exaggeration of white society, not realizing for some time that the Utkuhiksalingmuit had a very subtle and meaningful little word, takhaa, that followed "any comment that might possibly be construed as critical, hostile, plaintive or jealous." She had naturally thought that facial expression alone — the quizzically lifted eyebrow, the jolly laugh or some similar white accompaniment — made entirely clear the fact that the comment *was* funny–ha-ha and not funny-peculiar. As a great deal of teasing goes on in Eskimo families — often as a subtle form of tuition of children — some of her reciprocal efforts, unqualified by takhaa, must have sounded alarmingly offensive; it would be like playing the Eskimo equivalent of "Here comes a candle to light you to bed, and here comes a chopper to chop off your head" with a child, and really meaning it.

One shudders now at the literal impact of other white niceties of conversational exchange, such as "I could have murdered you with pleasure" (when I found you'd taken all the bath water), or even "My feet are killing me." (Not long ago I heard a mother of my acquaintance say of her six-month-old son, "He's so heavenly I could *eat* him.")

It is strange that we, with our centuries of developing the more civilized overtones of communication, have no clearly defined equivalent of takhaa and must depend on a primitive mobility of features, verbal inflection, or, as in so many instances of conversation today, unliteral, grossly exaggerated or unrelated statements to express our real disassociation from meaning.

Something else clicked into place over language, after hearing of a question put by Annaviapik that had puzzled Hugh: "Are you afraid of us?" Twice on separate occasions I had had that same question put to me by Indians and had been puzzled too. Once was in a rice-gatherer's camp; they were having a windup powwow that night, a jollification, and asked if we would like to stay for it. Part of me wanted to very much, the other part knew that the beer would flow freely, that the lake would have to be crossed in the darkness, and that the evening might well end in a familiar pattern of a black eye or two, or some passed-out reveler being fished out of the lake. So, regretfully, we declined. "Are you afraid of us?" asked one man, laughing, and I denied it with genuine astonishment, for fear had no part in the refusal — it was just common sense. But the question nagged my mind on the way back; had he, with some unusual percipience, seen me conjuring up the punchups and the passing out, but interpreted them as a fear of assault on myself? And if so, had I something to be afraid of? Was my lack of fear ethnic ignorance or naïveté?

Some months later I was asked into an Indian shack on a not particularly salubrious reserve, but declined (because I had just shut the car door on my fingers, as a matter of fact, and felt a bit sick), and the Indian with me asked, "Are you afraid of them?" There was no point in telling him that the only thing I was afraid of was passing out on the floor of the shack, because his reaction on opening the car door to free the crushed fingers had been a good hearty laugh; I didn't feel like talking, so I just said "Yes." "You must not be afraid," he said, and added, "I shall be there." The fact that he was a head shorter than myself didn't make his comment any less gallant, so I couldn't offend, and in I went — and spent two dreadful hours drinking tea in a stuffy smelly house with a group of people who sounded impassioned enough to be planning an uprising, but who were actually thrashing out who should pay for Joe Wild Potato's false teeth if he got them. But the nagging puzzle reoccurred: what *should* I have been afraid of? What sort of mayhem did he think I thought might be committed along with the tea?

The answer to all this is now so glaringly obvious, since Hugh has confirmed that it is the same in the Eskimo language: substitute the word "shy" for "afraid" and you have it. Shyness is a form of fear, and there are many manifestations of fear that our language does not define as such; somewhere along the translating line of the centuries some subtlety of usage had been missed, some cultural barrier left unsurmounted. One wonders how many other, more far-reaching, misunderstandings have occurred this way.

How can we not offend a people unaccustomed to such methods of communication, as did Jean Briggs so unwittingly, as any of us might do, who *think* we are bending over backward to achieve rapport? I think, in that context, of the giggling common to both Indian and Eskimo women; it is their invariable response to a first meeting, to such mundane (to us) questions as "Do you like it?" "How much do I owe you?" "Would you like a cup of coffee?" or "What a lovely day!" After a while it becomes contagious: there we all are, giggling away like mad, they possibly from embarrassment, pleasure or shyness; but I am of another culture, where giggling is associated with fun — and youthful fun at that — so how do I know that *my* rusty efforts are not being misinterpreted, that possibly *my* social response should be a silent smile, a deprecating chuckle (difficult this one: I've just tried it, and it sounded maniacal), or even a reassuring handshake? One cannot help wondering how it could ever be possible to achieve complete natural emotional rapport with another ethnic group, unless some essential understanding were imprinted on one at the critical infantile stage, or one were subjected to some form of total brainwashing and started all over again.

The laughter invariably commented upon by all who write about Eskimos (giving rise to the impression sometimes that all Eskimos live in a state of perpetual merriment) is more likely to be, as Jean Briggs shrewdly observed, "an easy and all em-

bracing way of dealing with the unusual situation." This probably goes for social giggling, too.

But even laughter can have its dangers of misinterpretation,
as Colly Scullion once found when they were stationed in Clyde
River and she was pregnant with Christopher. One of their
childless Eskimo friends there pointed out one day that she
had many more fecund years ahead of her, while his Annatoolia
no longer had any hope, and so he suggested that they should
have whatever Colly produced this time. Colly naturally thought
that this was a joking remark, and simply laughed. Unfortunately
laughter can also mean, if not actually assent, at least that no
objection is raised to a proposal. When she returned from Montreal with her brand-new son, Annatoolia's husband came hot-
footing up with the present of a walrus carving, all set to take the
baby home with him. He was very offended when Colly refused
to part with Christopher, accusing her of breaking her word, and
refusing to speak to or acknowledge her for weeks afterward.

By now I had heard plenty of similar anecdotes and experiences of similar misinterpretations between the Inuit and the
Kabloonah, for naturally the Inuit, as individuals and as a people, were a topic of endless and sincerely concerned conversation. Voiced often enough in newspaper articles and magazines
in the south, there was the broad general concern over progress
bringing civilization's problems, its misfires, mistakes, sicknesses
and catastrophes, too early, too often, and too heavily for the
ingestion of aboriginal "children." Even its so-called benefits
(decreased mortality, increased age expectation, warmth, and
lack of hardship or financial worry) might turn into eventual
hazards of laziness and greed, loss of skills, and eventually loss
of racial pride.

Then there were the other usual problems of an emergent
society, but more local ones: how much to give or withhold of
self-administration or material necessities; how far to take over

the welfare of the children, with school meals, once-a-week showers, curfews, etc., and equate it with the ultimate weakening of family responsibility; and then the invariable great unanswerable question at the end: *What to do with the educated product at the end of it all!*

This of course, to me listening, sounded like the usual conversation concerning the emergent generation of white society (where Ph.D.s are already a surplus on the job market): too much is done for them, so that they no longer have to think for themselves, and come to rely on government assistance for almost everything, feeling that they have somehow been cheated if they don't get it.

But at least at home I could listen to the point of view of the subjects, and discuss it with them. Here it was entirely a one-sided presentation. Hugh Brody had already found a sophistication of thought that might surprise the Territories administration, in particular an unexpectedly sympathetic understanding of the problems and frustrations often imposed upon local administrators by those immediately above on the government ladder. But I doubt if there are many white people, save those who have married Eskimos, or have spent so much of their life among them that they are totally fluent in conversation (and outlook), who have won a true reciprocity of thought and discussion.

This was not for want of trying; that there was friendship, and genuine admiration — even envy sometimes — of many aspects of Eskimo life, the closeness of family life in particular, was obvious; that there was occasional exasperation or frustration was equally and inevitably obvious. This was normal and to be expected; but I often had an uneasy feeling that Kabloonah reality was sometimes blurred by what I can only describe as Teddy Bear — or Edwardee Nanook — thinking mixed up with a mistaken tendency to parallel emergent problems with those of the northern Indians. Mistaken, I feel, because except for a few fatal contretemps with the earliest explorers, the Eskimos, never a warring person anyway, was never "the enemy" to the first invaders of his limitless (and unenviable) land; as the Indian, fiercely defending his highly desirable territory, so soon became. Far from being the savage opposition to be suppressed at all costs, the Eskimo was the indigenous help without whom the white explorer could not have survived. On closer acquaintance he became a figure greatly to be admired, endearing and jolly, showing superlative ingenuity and endurance; and later he evolved into the more public image of a small, quaint, furry, yet heroic figure against his white wilderness. *Nanook of the North*, that superb documentary, set a prototype that has endured to this day. But if we are not careful with our thinking he could too easily become Edwardee Nanook, stuffed with sawdust, a label saying Made in Canada sewn on his paws, sitting forever on a dusty shelf because the children who loved him once still like to think wistfully of him there, preserved and safe for all time even though they themselves have long grown up.

This original meeting of the admirable Eskimo with the white man eliminates the hereditary hang-up of the defeated, often territorially cheated Indian, still nursing an underdog grievance, belatedly raising his voice in a protest that too often comes over to white ears as a whine instead. However equal or superior the northern Ojibwa or Cree (many of whom are Arctic inhabitants) may feel himself to be amongst his own people in private it is not usually apparent in his public relationships with the white man.

But the bearing of the average Eskimo against his own background in the eastern Arctic is very different: friendly and polite, tolerant, yet reserved; one of self-assurance in fact.

I also felt, more and more strongly, that there was also a subtle mixture of indifference and indulgence toward white mores and eccentricities: something that I couldn't quite pin down, but that reminded me somehow of the lesser lynx's attitude:

> *The laughter of the Lesser Lynx*
> *Is often insincere;*
> *It pays to be polite, he thinks,*
> *If Royalty is near.*
> *So when the Lion steals his food*
> *Or kicks him from behind,*
> *He smiles, of course — but, oh, the rude*
> *Remarks that cross his mind!*
> — E. V. Ruan, *Cuckoo Calling*

Thirty years ago Rasmussen observed that he had learned from an old Eskimo, "It is generally believed that white men have quite the same minds as small children. Therefore one should always give way to them. They are easily angered, and when they cannot get their will they are moody, and like children, have the strangest ideas and fancies" — a somewhat sobering estimate, and one that time does not seem to have modified.

When one considers that curious and discerning word *ihuna* that so nebulously yet firmly separates the sheep from the goats, the reasons for our classification become clearer. Ihuma applies to those who are unaware of their responsibility for their actions to the human race, such as small children, the mentally ill, or dogs — all those that give way to immature emotions, such as bad temper or frustration or aggression, which are otherwise stringently condemned. Children grow out of this, so might the mentally ill, but dogs never do. Dogs can be bad-tempered and aggressive, and they make no attempt to suppress these qualities — qualities which many Kabloonahs make no attempt to suppress either. Hence the belief of the Utkuhiksalingmuit, formed from decades of observing Kabloonah behavior in general, that we must be of canine descent.

Were it not for the fact that we show some human attributes we would be out of the running entirely for the possession of qualities that inspire *nakli* feelings: another equally discerning word that Jean Briggs found in use among the Utkuhiksalingmuit.

I think their ethical logic is something like this: human beings are defined as beings-to-be-nurtured (*nakli*); such nurturant feelings and behaviour are the antithesis of hostile feelings and behaviour. This interpretation, I think, is supported by the fact that the Utkuhiksalingmuit do direct both physical and verbal aggression towards dogs, who are *not* defined as beings-to-be-nurtured (*nakli*).

Hence the borderline doubt as to whether we can aspire to nakli status, being "in their view about as bad tempered as the dogs from whom we are descended," or remain immature *ihuna*, forever unnurtured, with Beware of the Dog branded on our scowling foreheads.

(This knowledge can have a decidedly inhibiting effect, I found. Never again will I give the refrigerator an exasperated kick to stop its vibrations, nor will I snarl aggressively at the driver who has just pinched my parking place, without an uneasy feeling that my rising hackles and laid-back ears are clearly visible. Nor will I hop around uttering profanities at whoever has spilled the carpet tacks on the floor; nor . . . but name the emotion, and I find that we demonstrate it outwardly every day. No wonder we don't inspire nakli feelings. No wonder the Eskimo equivalent to "If you don't behave the Policeman/Bogeyman/Doctor-with-a-big-needle will come and get you" is "The Kabloonah will adopt you.")

Alcohol and its concomitant problems was another subject that cropped up frequently, usually following speculation on

what would happen to Pond when the iron ore development at
Mary Lake opened up. Under the Northwest Territories law an
annually increasing percentage of indigenous labor must be
used on any such project, and Pond Inlet would be the nearest
large source on which to draw. This would mean a further
breakup of the family pattern if the men went to work there, or
the creation of an artificial company settlement if their wives
accompanied them, or possibly a great increase in population at
Pond if a training center were established there. With high
wage packets and liquor more easily available, either place
might well turn into the hell's half-acre type of town that
Frobisher Bay became when the American Air Command station was established there.

All this was speculation. What was fact to me was that the
first year I had written in my journal:

Alcohol does not seem to be a problem here (at least on the surface).
Am told that there is only a small hard core of drinkers, consisting
originally of only the men who were regularly employed and therefore
had the money to indulge; originally the wives would have no part in
it, but latterly, apparently, a few have joined in. But as a whole men
will go out to Frobisher, Resolute or further south, for months possibly, and be exposed to pubs, etc., yet return here totally unaffected.

But when I returned the following year there was one charm-
ing, attractive young woman, the mother of two children, no
longer there:

. . . in March, after a "party," she had left to walk home through the
village; no one missed her, for D (her husband) thought she had gone
with someone else and someone else no doubt thought she was with
him (I gather no one was in much of a condition to think anyway).
Next morning she was found frozen to death — her tracks showed
that she had just walked in circles, not more than a hundred yards
from her house. It was a ghastly shock to the whole community. J

tried to drive a lesson home by having an Adult Education officer come up and give some lectures on the evils of drink, etc. — these attended by full houses — but says he doesn't think it will have much effect.

That same year just after Christmas, Soolah's half brother, Henry Tualuardjuk, one of the best carvers at Pond, killed his own son with an ax. So alcohol has already taken its toll in Shangri-La.

Yet I cannot help thinking that it is not only useless but presumptuous for white people to attempt to deal with this problem or adopt an overprotective policy as a solution; Tremblay's remark that "the Eskimo has little to learn from the white man" is only too true, for after all our centuries of experience, with the use and abuse, the problem, when it exists, remains individual. Some people get drunk or become alcoholics, some people drink and become neither; some people don't drink at all: it is another form of the survival of the fittest. We can tell them what we know (but in humility), make literature available, train adult education officers to lecture, but in the end it is the Eskimo himself who must deal with his own adjustment problems. There is no longer any time or room left for the singling out of ethnic groups for preservation or protection against themselves, when concerns for mankind's survival have become global. We are all, the sophisticated and the primitive, the exploiter and the exploited, caught up in the same machine. It is a hard and unpleasant fact, but the sooner we become objective about it the better.

I can't help feeling that the average Eskimo will do a far better job anyway of coping with the problems of civilization than we ourselves who created them; and that all aspects of self-destruction being equal, he stands a far greater chance of ultimate survival. He has adjusted to a technological age within a decade and, possibly most important, he enters that age with his backbone already stiffened genetically: "Few peoples in the world have been pressed to such limits of endurance or their ingenuity tested in a more challenging environment than the Eskimo." Given the time, therefore, it would seem that they have the inherent makings of being able to come to terms with yet another challenge.

He has been brought up too, since childhood, in the discipline of trial and error: it would be a very stupid child-grown Eskimo who did not soon realize that excess alcohol, drugs, or anything that causes a diminution of responsibility can never meet the Arctic on safe terms; to relax one's guard against the dangerous might of such an environment could be suicidal.

Such danger might well be the Eskimo's most meaningful safeguard, for I believe they love their mighty land and are so much a part of it, so indivisible, that they could not be happy for long anywhere else, whatever the dollar enticement of the south. I believe that one of two things may happen when the end comes: when his lands and seas can no longer support him the Eskimo will simply say, "Ajaqnak — ah, well, that's that," and become naturally extinct without further fuss or bother; or, should some cataclysm overtake the entire world, I cannot help thinking that the small, cheerful, resourceful and resolute figure of Edwardee Nanook might be the only one to rise from the ashes and start all over again.

Perhaps I am overoptimistic; perhaps if I return to Pond in five years' time I shall find cause to eat my words. Certainly it is one of the most idyllic communities in the eastern Arctic, and this must limit the worth of generalities. But other eastern Arctic communities are already aware of dangers, and are trying to deal with them, if the articles I read in the *Midnight Sun*, a paper produced in Igloolik, the nearest settlement to Pond, are anything to go by.

Apart from local items of news or decisions taken by the

council (such as the decision to ban the use of skidoos after
11 P.M. — a fantastically forward decision when one thinks of
the incessant noise of engines that the average white suburb
puts up with at all hours — "unless if ungert [sic] things happen, or if they come from hunting it's O.K."), there were some
very shrewd and pertinent articles on such subjects as adult
education and the workings of the Co-op, and a long editorial
summing up the findings of a recent conference on alcohol.
This set out very realistically the dangers of the *abuse* of alcohol and included this statement:

. . . liqour destorys body just like the drugs. Some of the drugs are
tea, coffee and cigarettes, but these are not dangerous. Some people
use liqour as a drug and it's okay if you don't use them too much.
Some people could drink lots of liqour and not get drunk and others
with small amount of liqour, they'd get drunk. After they sobored up
they become sick. This is the worst part of drinking. Liqour destorys
body and mind. It even kills people, if they're drunk and get mad they
could kill any person. They do wrong things not knowing what they
are doing because they are out of their minds.

It ended with this comment concerning the question of the
future sale of liquor in settlements:

It is more dangerous to try and stop the liqour. Lots of people want
liqour in their places but others don't. For sure the liqour will be
coming to settlements. If the people don't want it to come to their
places, other people might start making home brew and maybe it
would cause death to some of them.

I also liked the plea for more people to make use of the adult
education facilities offered and not say "I can not learn any
more because I am too old to learn." The answer to this was

You older people learn something every day by doing something and
watching others. I have seen older people fixing their skidoos inside

and out. The skidoo has been in existence only for a few years. This proves you could learn something.

Also under education came the answer to "How come teachers always fussy when my child is late to go to school in the morning?" After pointing out that "teachers fussy" for the very good reason that they have the ultimate benefit of the child in mind, the writer goes on to say:

Your child's education depends on the teacher but much more on you, as a parent, because you are the boss for your child, nobody else. You must see that your child gets to school on time, has a good rest at night and if old enough to have homework that it gets done.

Finally, I cannot resist quoting what was to me the most telling and hopeful paragraph of all:

In the past, Inuit often have agreed whenever Qallunaaq [white authority is meant here] said or suggested something without really realising or thinking it over what they are agreeing about. This must not CONTINUE if you are to make more decisions and take more responsibilities in your Community.

While Igloolik was Pond's nearest comparably sized neighbor (about three hundred miles away), it was as different as chalk is from cheese. When I went there, by a lucky lift in an Otter chartered for some surveyors, the pilot's pipe appeared round the cockpit soon after takeoff, and he addressed his five passengers in a nice parody of the giant airline pilot's spiel: "We will be flying at an approximate height of 10,000 feet for Igloolik — if I can find it in these clouds. Approximate flying time, two, three or four hours. We hope you will enjoy your flight with us, and if you want anything — get up and get it!"

I could understand his difficulty about finding Igloolik when it eventually appeared:

It was just a flat sandy swirl, with no vegetation whatsoever, lying off Melville Island, the center of the walrus hunting area. I would go mad if I lived there: nowhere to go, just walking round and round a small sandbar. Yet when we had rattled into the settlement, crammed into a Bombadier like sardines, I saw that the seemingly flat desolation from the air had a beauty of its own, something to do with the austerity contrasting with a soft translucent pink-pearly sheen on the still water.

There were other differences, one of the most striking being the almost mathematical division of the island between the two churches, Anglican and Catholic — almost, as someone said, as though a line had been drawn across the pebbly beach. The Catholic church dominated the scene if only in sheer uniqueness:

It is a fascinating place, built by Father Fournier's hands alone in limestone blocks. The handle of the porch door, the outer one, was made from walrus bone, the center timbers of the door set in the shape of a cross, and closing with a weighted whisper before the inner insulating door. Inside was a beautiful low arched ceiling, dark and simple, and the westering sun streaming through stained glass windows — which on closer inspection turned out to be made of plastic. A komatik raised on bone supports made the low altar, the six candleholders formed from inverted walrus tusks. Before it, the head lying beyond the shallow step, was an enormous polar bear skin, the hind legs stretching back to the altar. There were sealskin kneelers, with beautiful inset work. All the windows, small and deeply set, had "stained glass" portraying realistically leaded stories from the New Testament, the figures all Eskimo — a hunter, a woman with a child in her amouti, a carver — and the text below in Eskimo syllabics.

It was beautifully designed and executed, the recurring use of walrus (for a walrus-hunting congregation) most ingenious, and it was a very moving monument to the long years of love and labor that Father Fournier had put into it. It had a wonderfully peaceful atmosphere, but somehow, as I stood there in the utter silence of its deep insulation, trying to take it all in, all I could think of was Rasmussen's description of Au's extraneous carving of his walrus episode, mixed up with a sudden vision of Koonah's flattened cigarette package fan on her wall at Pond: the imposition of white ideas of what constituted a place of worship in the Arctic to be attended by a congregation largely made up of walrus hunters (male) and their wives and families.

The people seemed more sophisticated in keeping, most of them wearing store-bought clothes; the teen-agers — a delightful friendly lot, not a bit shy, and far more outgoing than their Pond contemporaries — were dressed for the most part in western fashion, cowboy hats and Levis, and all spoke surprisingly colloquial English. Only the beach, littered with blubber and bones and oil drums, seemed familiar, and the huskies' music, although here on this small island it seemed more overwhelming. There were at least fifty of them staked out closely together beyond the fishing boats, all shapes and sizes and colors, even down to quite young pups, all in full voice.

Arctic Bay, about three hundred miles due west, was actually the nearest community to Pond, but it was little more than a handful of houses scattered along the shores of a wide beautiful bay beneath a sweeping half moon of hills: a nursing station, a school, half an acre of oil barrels, and a hair-raising airstrip running parallel to the shore and looking more like a cart track than anything else.

Two or three flying hours beyond that to the northwest on Cornwallis Island, close to the north magnetic pole, was Resolute Bay, where once a week a jet arrived via Frobisher Bay from Montreal, nearly two thousand miles away. Resolute was the base for most of the flying operations in the eastern Arctic, although one could not help wondering why it had been so specifically chosen, as there seemed to be a perpetually low cloud ceiling there. It was a bleak place, just two rows of joined Quonset huts facing one another on the edge of the field: one set of huts with official offices, the RCMP post, and the cinema; the other consisting entirely of the government-run "Tower Foundation," the only place to stay for transients or workers, with an enormous cafeteria, recreation rooms, and cell-like bedrooms with the windows eight feet up. It was like a super YMCA hostel, the only difference being the presence of a bar and the price, which was superlative. The only road led to the small Eskimo village two miles away. A fate worse than death, going or coming from Pond, was to be socked in at Resolute; and one invariably was. Apart from the nightly movie there was nothing else to do but retire to bed and read one's way through the endless paperbacks left in the room by other wayfarers and rise only to eat.

This one did conscientiously, whether one was hungry or not, for three meals a day, at five dollars a meal, were charged whether one ate them or not; and that, plus fifteen dollars a day for the room, made one determined to get one's money's worth — as a taxpayer at least, for one's checks were made out to the Receiver General of Canada. Besides, the food was excellent. We presented something of a problem, the place being run on men-only lines; an entire set of washrooms was once decorously labeled "Ladies Only" for our benefit. However, some unknown hand very sensibly removed the sign after a few hours.

The only other interesting feature of Resolute was that it was the base of Atlas Aviation, the "bush plane" company started by Wendell Phipps some twenty years before, whose history is synonymous with the development of the eastern Arctic, a company that has had so many decades of accident-free flying that they have the lowest insurance rates of any aviation company in Canada. And this despite the fact that they operate in what must be the most rugged flying terrain with the most rapidly changing weather conditions in the world—plus a few local peculiar features, such as total darkness for half the year and the proximity of the north magnetic pole to foul up the compasses of small aircraft. Weldy Phipps has deservedly become a giant even in the legendary company of the bush pilots of Canada.

Resolute was also the home of Markoosie, the pilot who worked for Weldy Phipps, the first Eskimo to appear in my journal that first year, and a living example of all that is best in the modern Eskimo. Small and slight, he looked about nineteen, but was in fact twenty-seven and the father of four children. He is in every sense of the word a successful Eskimo: successful not only in his indigenous world, but in the white man's world, completely fluent in both languages. After years of hunting, he returned to school to get the requisite education that would enable him to leave his homeland and his family for a year while he took his pilot's license thousands of miles south, first a private one and then the commercial license that enabled him to join Atlas Aviation. In the interim between our first meeting and my return the following year he wrote a novel, *Harpoon of the Hunter*, which rapidly became a best seller and was translated into six languages. This year he was appointed to the board of Panarctic Oils Limited. Such success could well go to the head of any young man: Markoosie remains as natural and unaffected as ever, totally unspoiled by financial success, deeply religious, a hunter from this most primitive land taken as naturally to the skies as the Ookpik, the snowy owl of his people.

Some six hundred miles away on the southernmost tip of Baffin was Frobisher Bay, the "capital" of the eastern Arctic — "Frob" to those who live in the north. To a newcomer, who had known only the simplicity and peace of remote, naturally established settlements, Frob was a revelation of ingenuity, incongruity, some admiration and much horror. The sprawling ugly "city" sprang into being out of the wilderness during the last war, when the United States Strategic Air Command chose the site. It has the second longest natural runway on the north American continent: nine hundred feet.

The first one saw of Frob from the air was the quite amazing sight of an eight-story apartment building towering solitary out of a barren wilderness over a cluster of small buildings and oil barrels. Having landed and rattled off "downtown" in a taxi, one's immediate impression was of the littered squalor "civilization" brings to the Arctic:

Oil drums, oil drums everywhere; no wonder Prince Philip said it was just one great big garbage dump. A remark that has not endeared him to the local potentates, I gather. There are reminders all over of the recent Royal visit — Union Jack still flying outside the Area Administrator's house, street signs newly painted, streets hastily tidied up.

So at least I saw Frob at its tidiest. Heaven knows what it was like before. To be fair, it is difficult to keep a city superficially tidy in the Arctic, with permafrost and graying snow, and even its most intimate innards exposed. The raised maze of the huge Utilidor pipes that carry sewage and water is a prominent feature. And because it was summer there was construction work going on everywhere.

The deserted U.S. base stands on top of the hill behind the town, a ghostly monument to the original city fathers, turned over to Canada when they left for the token payment of a dollar or so:

Difficult to judge how many millions of dollars thrown away when they left," I wrote in my journal after wandering the site, still surrounded by its towering fence, the catwalks on stilts in case of "whiteouts" still intact, the Operations Room with tiered seats just like the movies. "All electrical radio, radar, etc. equipment burned or hacked to pieces, shed after shed of twisted broken remains. The cars and trucks were put into gear and sent over the hill to the gravel pit below, then bulldozed over, so that no one could possibly benefit from them. Yet they left canteen furniture, bunks, etc. With such an example of white wastefulness to a people accustomed to making something out of nothing, everything out of something, perhaps it's small wonder that the Eskimos exposed to it were never the same again. They could be another race compared to Pond: clambering back through the town to the hotel over construction work, along the tops of the Utilidors, around the oil barrels, etc. there were small children asking for "pennies," tarty looking teenage girls emerging from the Palace Theatre — one memorable character with the shortest of sawn-off shorts, purple fish-net leotards and a small dirty baby in a filthy amouti on her back — puffy-eyed, flabby-faced boys shouting uninhibitedly Anglo-Saxon badinage after them, a distinct smell of hair tonic and/or vanilla essence wafting back as they opened their mouths. . . . There are few friendly open faces, healthy and clear-eyed, too many with the hateful, strained, almost furtive look that one has seen among Indians living on the white fringe. Yet I think the Skid Row Indian has more dignity than the Eskimo equivalent — perhaps the contrast is too sudden and unexpected here. Or the Arctic makes too pitiless a background for our human squalor? Whatever it is I *loathe* the place . . . want to bury my head in the permafrost and not see it, not believe it.

I must have been feeling very livery. There is plenty more in this vein which would be unfair to accent, for obviously there must be many good things about Frobisher Bay which one would not come across in only two days — particularly if one were not in a very receptive mood, which I quite obviously was not. The new residential high school to which the eastern Arctic children will go instead of Churchill, so far away and so foreign to them, was an impressive modern building, for one thing. So was the hotel. There was an excellent hospital. There *were* well-dressed decorous Eskimos in the huge hotel bar, which was decorated with murals by Mary Cousins, the Eskimo wife of one of the education officers; there *were* friendly people — I remember one woman in particular handing me her fishing rod while I was watching her casting for salmon from a rocky point. There *were* some working on construction, but if I noticed them it was because they were the exception. It seemed essentially a white people's town: from waiters to bulldozer operators, clerks to teachers, taxi drivers to hotel receptionists, with a fringe of Eskimos, looking as environmentally displaced as polar bears in a zoo, their lives and surroundings as contrived and artificial. The thought of the Pond Inlet children joining them for their most impressionable high school years made me cringe.

At least my jaundiced entries about Frob ended on a happier personal note:

Went out to Apex about three miles away; it was the original settlement, with Hudson Bay post and Anglican church (which the Queen attended on her visit, and spent her time slapping at mosquitoes). Much more peaceful out here, most of the houses have already been shifted, only a few inhabitants left, bitterly resenting their impending move into the squalor of Frobisher, but powerless to resist, as all necessary wintertime service will no longer operate — road clearance particularly important.

A large bearded character emerged out of a pleasant house, all its windows filled with flowers, and asked us to give him and his kayak a lift down to the Hudson Bay post, as he was going across the bay and up the river to deliver some caribou meat to an archaeologist camped out there. We loaded the homemade kayak, frail and decked with thin linoleum, on the truck and drove down to the sandy beach before the store. There he suggested that I might like to cross the bay with him; he would drop me off on the peninsula and I could walk back alone and be picked up by the truck eventually, just giving me nice time to catch the plane at noon.

The words were hardly out of his mouth before I had borrowed a sweater and was aboard. I took a paddle, twin bladed, and found the rhythm almost effortless once one had learned to push the alternate blade instead of traditionally pulling the one in the water. So peaceful and pleasant after the rattling truck and Frobisher and I began to feel restored. We crossed the bay in about twenty minutes, heading for the ships anchored out, skirted the ice floes off the point of the peninsula, then through an open path between little bergers, then up by the mouth of the river. Here he dropped me off. I thanked him. "When I saw you I knew you'd be the sort of person who'd like to come," he said and paddled off — leaving me wondering (still) whether it was a compliment or an assessment of my sanity. His "ten minute walk" back along the peninsula turned out to be a frightening half hour scramble over the rocks, including an almost vertical ascent by the pipe line. Frightening, not so much from fear of dropping the heavy camera as of missing the plane and having to spend another 24 hours there.

I had acquired some blisters on the palms of my hands from the paddle. One of them became infected, leaving — not inappropriately — a small scar which still remains. But whether to remind me of Frobisher Bay or as a warning not to indulge in Teddy Bear thinking, I don't know.

୬୬ *Chapter 10* ୬୬

As the summer progressed the sound of skidoos was replaced by outboard engines, and sometimes I went to sleep with the sound of ice-free waves lapping below my window; but there was so much to do, such a short season, that I almost grudged the time asleep: trying to master a new string game, catching up with the wild flowers, fishing, or sealing.

As there had been activity on the ice before, now it was on the long sandy beach before the settlement. One afternoon, sitting there watching Kyak paint his large fishing boat in preparation for his annual sealing expedition, the sand was so warm, the sun so brilliant, the water so blue, that if it had not been for the occasional whiff of a rotting narwhal carcass nearby it could have been the South of France.

That was a wonderful afternoon, for presently, down the steep embankment, came Martha and Inoogah's two-year-old daughter, Isshtee, with plump Koopah, whom I knew from the kindergarten, and a thin little friend about seven years old. They were all in white amoutis, even tiny Isshtee, and were obviously playing Mothers, with dolls in their hoods and carrying handbags. At least, the two bigger girls had dolls; little Isshtee had a tightly rolled-up towel instead for a make-believe

doll and no handbag. I had the movie camera with me and pretended to be using it, to their self-conscious delight, but I was
really only letting the batteries make the appropriate noise and
not shooting any film. When the novelty had worn off and they
were playing naturally, I let the film go through. Before I knew
where I was I had shot nearly three rolls, for they were such a
delight to watch. Soon a small brother arrived to sail his boat
on the end of a string; then Billy, the adopted son of Merkasiak
from the Hudson Bay post — half white and the terror of Pond
Inlet apparently — throwing a harpoon across the sand to at-
tract attention. The little girls, with studious disapproval,
ignored him.

The older girls were very careful, loving mothers. Little
Isshtee tried to follow the pattern, but every now and then she
grew bored and put the feeding bottle in her own mouth, or
absent-mindedly dropped the baby in the sand, once even un-
rolling the poor child to make a little tent for herself. The thin
little girl's doll was bottle-fed too, but Koopah belonged to the
natural school: her doll was shoved down the front of her
amouti and invited to partake from a realistically twisted-up
piece of dress. Once it was presumably satisfied and settled
down, Koopah rocked back and forth with as much maternal
aplomb as if she were twenty-seven and the mother of five instead of seven years old. Fresh diapers were brought out from
the handbags, the doll children changed, then each child
helped the other slip its baby into the amouti hood. This put
ideas into Isshtee's head — not too long out of the amouti herself, and rather sleepy, it must have seemed a very desirable
place to be — she howled. The others soothed her maternally
and she started up the steep hillside for home, but slipped and
sobbed, so the thin little girl went to her aid, and laughing
gently, pulled her up. In the meantime Koopah was busy making
a tent house — a long stick propped against a boat and a sheet

draped over; she retired in there, presumably to cook her husband's dinner, and presently the other little girl joined her inside, the tent heaving and bulging with much giggling.

Soon after, on that same wonderful warm afternoon, the figure of Colly appeared on the beach, so small that she could be taken for an Eskimo woman — particularly when she had Christopher in her amouti — and it was always something of a shock to see the very fair hair instead, and the almost lint-white head of Christopher sticking out of the hood. Then John arrived, and we pushed out the big gray government canoe to try out the brand-new outboard. We ran down to the Salmon River close to the coast at first, then farther out, by little bergers massing before the entrance to Janes Creek, until we came to the open waters of the big river and landed on a sandy spit. Annakudlip was there, setting nets with the help of his daughter, Esther, and another young girl. He had about eight nice fish in the bottom of the boat from the last haul, beautiful clean-run Arctic char, and was cleaning them then and there in the water, standing ankle deep in his sealskin kamiks. Other fishermen were there too, coming and going, for once the nets were set they turned the boats toward the massed ice beyond and went off hunting seal. It was very peaceful on the sandy spit, with the river sounds and a gentle warm wind. I walked around the narrow neck to the mainland: where the tussocks of purple-blue grass began there were random carpets of blue sandwort pressed close to the sand, and hundreds of brittle-shelled mussel halves, tiny gnarled branches of willow driftwood, and sometimes a sand-smoothed piece of komatik runner washed up on the shore.

An Arctic tern hovered like a hummingbird above an upended chunk of ice close to shore, then dived, slicing into the water like a knife. Close by on a rock, peeping hungrily, was the baby, and the parent fed it; then back to the watchful hovering. A little flock of red-breasted phalarope busied themselves at the water's edge, the first I had seen. At a distance I had taken them for sanderlings. They were pretty little birds, like toys, the female so much more striking for once, and even more toylike in the water, like miniature gulls. They were quite unafraid, and I walked up to within a few yards before they took to the water, riding there about ten feet out, and watching me with soft incurious eyes.

Annakudlip had a caribou skin and a piece of canvas spread out on the sand, so we sat or lay around as he boiled up a pan of tea, talking lazily, while young Christopher poured sand over people from a mug, and no one minded. Annakudlip gravely put on a cowboy hat belonging to one of the girls, nodding his head, the charms on the looped-up chin strap dangling in front of his nose, so that he looked even more like a nice brown Portuguese monkey than ever. The girls smiled indulgently ("Daddy being the Funny Man"). Young Christopher, admonished and admired with equal understanding in Eskimo or English, went too far with the sand game, had the mug removed and howled with fury. It was like any beach picnic anywhere in the world, without the sandy ham sandwiches — a strip of boiled muktuk took their place.

Then we thought we would go farther up the river to see how many nets had been set, but the engine had retired into sulky balkiness. John pulled and pulled, Annakudlip pulled, we all pulled — but not a spark. Finally one of the hunters' boats came in, moored alongside, and this time there was some more masterful tinkering with innards and pulling. When the engine did start we were afraid to stop it and piled in pretty quickly, for the tide had turned and the wind changed, so that all the open water before the bay at Pond was now a mass of shifting icepans with navigable leads opening and closing in minutes. Twice we tried to get through and twice had to retreat and make a detour; and for the first time I realized how quickly one could become trapped or nipped by the ice, and why people use small light canoes here — they can be slid over the ice to the next patch of open water. But our boat was too big for this. The third time round — it reminded me of trying to find one's way around the twisting lanes of Cornwall during the war when the signposts were removed — a new narrow road-lead opened up leading to open water and the beach. Far out by the iceberg we could see one boat inching along too late, for the channel out there had closed up; the men would probably haul the boat back over the ice, or get the stove out and make tea and settle down for the next wind change. We hoped it wasn't the boat with the children in it, for they had left earlier with one of the hunters.

On the way up the beach we saw them already at the window. Colly apologized for the engine's behavior and that we hadn't done any of the things we had planned, like exploring the upper reaches of the river. "I'm afraid it must have been very boring," she said, and astonished, I reassured her: far from being boring it had been a wonderful day, another day of peaceful timeless pottering, of warm content. No one could ask for more.

But that night, leaning out of my beloved window, following the long low silvery path of the sun across the maze of half-submerged ice and water to the dark mass of the Bylot range, now sharply etched, I saw that there was a different light over the ice to the west: it was almost mauve, and even as I watched the shimmering path vanished as the sun dipped momentarily behind the highest mountain. I had not realized how low its arc had become. And as though to emphasize it further, at that moment the shabby little bitch who had managed to evade authority and produce her litter deep under the schoolhouse trotted down the slope below, followed by her two surviving children: only a few days ago, it seemed, they had been furry balls,

stumbling around the entrance to their lair — now, to my astonishment, they were nearly as big as their mother. Time was flying by, and still I had not seen what I longed to see, the migrat-
ing narwhal, a narwhal hunt. I seemed doomed to miss it. A few
nights before three had passed directly under the window, but
were gone, in a slow lazy swirl, almost before I had had time to
register what they were.

Then fate was abundantly kind: almost the last entry in my
journal was:

Sunday — the last Sunday. A most wonderful day — warm and calm
and beautiful; three wishes granted — and without any of the usual
preliminary tedium of being kind to frogs or carrying little old ladies
over turbulent rivers either.

The first wish was to go back to the Bylot breeding grounds
and see this year's crop of the greater snow goose. It had not
seemed possible, as time was getting so short, and Doug Heyland was not camped on Bylot; the last time I had seen him was
when he appeared in a helicopter on Button Point. Then he
suddenly appeared that last Sunday, as though summoned out
of the blue, in an Atlas Aztec, with Jack Warner as pilot. He
was to finish the photographic survey for the year, and I spent
the afternoon with them. Not over Bylot, however, as that area
had already been covered — in one of their occasional inexplicable area changes none of the nesting pairs returned to last
year's site — but above the northeast area of the Boothia Peninsula, the most northerly point of the Canadian mainland, which
was more exciting anyway.

We flew at 2,000 feet, up and down, up and down what I
supposed were the grid lines of the periscope affair mounted
between the seats in the cockpit; the camera, a huge Leica, was
mounted on a hatch in the belly of the Aztec and somehow or

other connected with the periscope. Looking down, it was possible to distinguish individual geese, even goslings and the
gray of yearling birds, the flightless, unmated ones in their neat
tight white circles on lakes, or clustered thickly along river
banks. Doug estimated one such flock to have about seven hundred birds in it.

We passed and repassed the lower of the two ice caps, nearly
twelve miles across, purest white, only the terminal edges
stained as they melted into the mountainside, like a high white
mushroom. The ranges here, the shapes, the incredible flinging
around of every known geological form, were almost too much
to take in; even after seeing them again and again as we followed the grid, each time from a slightly different angle, it
seemed in the end impossible to believe them.

We had a mailbag on board for Father Mary, containing not
only his mail but items that he had requested in his last radio
link — tape cassettes, lard, magazines, etc. — so when the last
grid line was finished we flew a short distance up the coast of
Navy Board Inlet, and there, just past the first sandspit on the
next point, were the three tiny tents of Father Mary, Bob and
Jobee. We flew low over, to estimate for the drop, and three
little figures emerged from the tents. Then Jack shoved the mailbag, weighted with a brick, through his little inset window,
hanging onto it with a cord, waiting for the right moment. But
the bag filled up like a balloon, the tremendous drag of the
cord carved through Jack's hand, and with an anguished squeak
he let it go — and down went the mailbag straight into the sea.
It was about a hundred yards out, between the shore and the
ice, and at least it stayed afloat while we circled twice to mark
the spot while they got the boat out. But we could not wait any
longer to see what happened as the tank was getting low. Poor
Father always seemed to have the worst luck with maildrops:
the last one, aimed by John Scullion as he passed over in an

Otter, had landed far out on an icepan and was only retrieved days later. It had contained about six pounds of lard, wrapped in copies of *Time* magazine, and landed with such force that the lard went straight through the pages: they had had to throw in a page or two of *Time* every time they wanted to grease the frying pan, Father Mary had reported plaintively.

There was a gastronomic bonus to that day as well, for when we got back we ate the steaks issued to Doug by a kindly provisioning officer in Quebec. They were barbecued on the inverted top of the Scullions' new garbage can and were particularly superb after days of nothing but fish or seal. While we were eating we could see a flittering trail across the water below the windows, with hundreds of gulls and fulmars in its wake — shoals of silvery sprats. So we went off in the boat to investigate with a cloud of kittiwakes in attendance.

Then my second wish came true: to see the other side of the iceberg. Tonight there was open water right out of it, and we circled it in awe, for it really was a magnificent piece of ice architecture. On one side, the side I had looked at so often, it towered up and up against a brilliantly blue sky, sheer and glistening smooth, falling away at the other end into the enormous contours of a sphinx. The other side was as though an amphitheater had been cut out of it, with a wide stage and a sheer backdrop of sculptured ice; the spotlight effect of the low sun completed the illusion. Even as we drifted by, a flock of eiders, black-speckled against the white, went by on a chunk of ice like another boatload of spectators.

To add to the day, when we returned, John said that he had just spoken to Father Mary on the radio and that the mailbag had been recovered.

Then the third and most important wish: suddenly someone looking out of the window said "Narwhal, *narwhal!*" "*Narwhal?*" said Rick, taking straight off from his chair by the chess-

Index

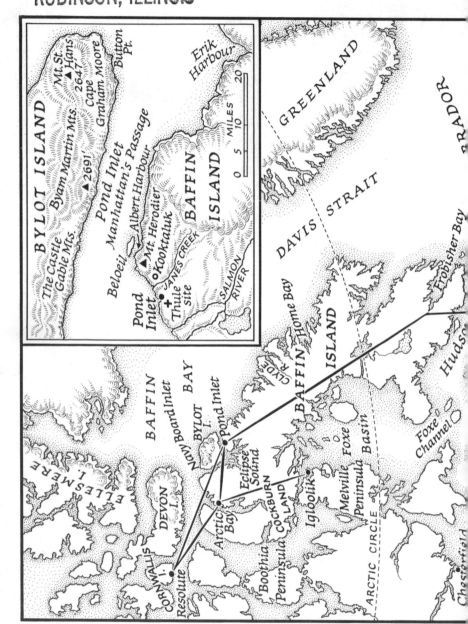